KINGDOM FAMILY DEVOTIONAL

52 WEEKS OF GROWING TOGETHER

TONY EVANS
and JONATHAN EVANS

TYNDALE HOUSE PUBLISHERS, INC.
CAROL STREAM, ILLINOIS

Library of Congress Cataloging-in-Publication Data

Names: Evans, Tony, date, author. | Evans, Jonathan, date, author.
Title: Kingdom family devotional : 52 weeks of growing together / Dr. Tony Evans and Jonathan Evans.
Description: Carol Stream, IL : Tyndale House Publishers, Inc., [2016]
Identifiers: LCCN 2016038908 | ISBN 9781589978553 (alk. paper)
Subjects: LCSH: Families—Religious life.
Classification: LCC BV4526.3 .E93 2016 | DDC 248.4—dc23 LC record available at https://lccn.loc.gov/2016038908

Printed in the United States of America

22   21   20   19   18   17
7   6   5   4   3

CONTENTS

INTRODUCTION

I f we're ever to see the salvation of our nation, we must first pursue the salvation of the family. The strength or weakness of the family will ultimately determine whether our society stands or falls. That's why we've written the *Kingdom Family Devotional.*

This devotional is designed to be a tool for you as parents to use with your children to instill biblical truth and spiritual values in the minds and hearts of the next generation. As the psalmist declared, "One generation shall praise Your works to another, and shall declare Your mighty acts" (Psalm 145:4, NASB).

This devotional tool has been developed around fifty-two themes to be covered, one per week, throughout the year. We have sought to communicate each theme in a way that's biblically sound and relevant. This book was also written with flexibility in mind, so that you can adapt the principles and projects to the various ages of your children. It's important to insert age-appropriate personal stories, illustrations, and applications as needed.

One of the best and most natural times to use these devotions is around the dinner table (Psalm 128:3) with the TV off and smartphones set aside. Having a concentrated time for the family to focus on God and one another is absolutely critical if we're going to overcome the secular, godless influences that are engulfing our children and drawing them away from the faith.

A suggested format is to begin and end each devotional time with prayer. This should include having the kids pray. You'll see that suggestions for prayers are included in some sessions, but most often you will be able to supply your own unique prayers.

To lead the family time, simply read each daily session aloud and follow any instructions that are italicized and enclosed in parentheses *(like this)*. It's always a good idea to privately read the session ahead of time. Each devotion has been written in first person for a parent to read aloud. If another family member reads the day's devotion, that person may need to modify some of the wording. Some sessions include easy activities that involve common household items. If you have those items ready in advance, your devotional time will unfold more smoothly. Sessions include Bible passages for you to read aloud, but do keep your own Bible nearby for reference.

Please note that on Wednesday a strong emphasis is placed on formal Bible study ("Wednesday in the Word"), while Friday focuses on fun projects for the weekend ("Fun Friday"). A variety of approaches will keep your family devotional time fresh and interesting. Feel free to adjust your approach to fit the needs of your family and the ages of your children. (For example, if your children are homeschooled, some of the references to classes and teachers may not apply.)

Finally, don't hesitate to offer small incentives for memorizing Scripture, learning concepts, and even teaching the lesson.

It's our desire to see your family thrive as you fulfill your primary role of guiding your children in a misguided world. Don't leave the spiritual development of your children to chance, TV, their peers, social media, the government, or even the church. The main responsibility for godly child-rearing belongs in the hands of parents (see Deuteronomy 6:1–9 and Psalm 144:12).

Our prayer is that these devotions will support your role in raising kingdom kids who learn to consistently live all of life under God's divine authority.

Tony Evans and Jonathan Evans

LOVE

Scripture Reading: John 3:16

Do you love chocolate cake? It's easy to say we love cake . . . or donuts . . . or fried chicken!

Love is a funny word, isn't it? We toss it around like a softball or baseball when we're playing catch. It goes from one thing to another easily. We love sports. We love our favorite TV shows. We love our favorite action heroes. We love our favorite food. We love that new girl or boy who just moved into town. We love playing video games, reading books, or skateboarding. You name it, and you'll hear someone say how much he or she loves it.

Did you know that God's definition of *love* isn't always like our own? When God talks about love, He isn't talking about ooey-gooey feelings we have somewhere in our hearts. He's talking about a commitment. He's talking about a choice. He's talking about putting someone else ahead of ourselves.

Love can be defined as "compassionately and righteously pursuing the well-being of another." Love is an action, not an emotion. And it's a responsibility God has commanded us to live out.

The apostle John tells us, "Dear friends, let us love one another, because love is from God, and everyone who loves has been born of God and knows God" (1 John 4:7).

Love is what we're to do. Be. Feel. And experience. Not just when something yummy pops out of the microwave or our favorite team wins the game. We'll talk more about love tomorrow. But for now, let's say 1 John 4:7 aloud enough times to learn it by heart. *(Start with short sections of the verse and add more until your family has memorized the whole passage.)*

LOVE

SCRIPTURE READING: JOHN 15:13

One day, out in the wilderness, a lioness was tending to her cubs. As she lay watching her precious cubs play, she spotted something sliding through the grass toward them. She stood up and trotted over to see what it was. As the lioness got closer, she realized that danger was approaching. A venomous snake was headed right toward the playing cubs, and it was getting ready to strike with a poisonous bite. The lioness loved her cubs and didn't want them hurt, so she attacked the snake to drive it away.

After a furious fight, the snake gave up and slithered away. What the lioness didn't realize is that she was bitten on her paw during the fight. The snakebite made her sick for a few days, but on the third day, she regained her full strength.

Let's talk about how this story reminds us of an important truth from the Word of God.

In what way is Jesus Christ like the lioness in the story? And how are we like the cubs? *(Encourage everyone to participate in the discussion.)*

Just as the lioness in the story was willing to sacrifice herself to save her cubs, Jesus died on the cross for our sins to keep us safe from Satan's evil plan. Jesus demonstrated His love for us through His sacrifice. Now we're free to live without worry or fear that death will "bite" us, because Jesus loved us so much that He took the bite for us.

Let's pray together and thank Jesus for loving us so very much.

LOVE

SCRIPTURE READING: 1 CORINTHIANS 13:4–8

God has an awful lot to say about love. In fact, it's one of the most popular topics in the Bible, mentioned almost three hundred different times. Now that's a lot of love!

During our time together today, let's look at what God says about love. We'll take turns reading the Scripture verses aloud together, and then we'll talk about them.

Love the Lord your God . . . [and] love your neighbor as yourself. There is no other command greater than these. MARK 12:30–31

Why do you think God said there's no other greater commandment?

Love is patient, love is kind. Love does not envy, is not boastful, is not conceited. 1 CORINTHIANS 13:4

What does it mean to be patient? Have you ever had to be patient with someone in our family or a friend? What happened?

Now these three remain: faith, hope, and love. But the greatest of these is love. 1 CORINTHIANS 13:13

What makes love so great?

There is no fear in love; instead, perfect love drives out fear. 1 JOHN 4:18

What are some things you're afraid of? How can love make those fears go away?

Greater love has no one than this, that one lay down his life for his friends. JOHN 15:13, NASB

Who laid down His life for His friends? How can we show love for our friends?

The one who does not love does not know God, for God is love. 1 JOHN 4:8, NASB

Is it possible to know God and not love others?

3

LOVE

SCRIPTURE READING: MARK 12:29–31

Love isn't simply something we feel for someone; it's something we're willing to demonstrate to someone no matter how we feel. Let's take a look at what we're learning about love and put it into action. First, each of us will go around the room and tell other family members that we love them and why. Next, each of us will choose one other family member and show love for that person this week by doing one special act of service every day.

You can choose to do the same act of service every day or something different. The goal is to do something you'd rather not do. Offer to do an act of service that will be a *sacrifice* for you.

(As family members decide on their acts of service, write them down on a large piece of paper. Label it "The Love Chart" and hang it where everyone can see it during the week.)

LOVE

SCRIPTURE READING: 1 JOHN 4:8

It's been great learning about love this week, hasn't it?
Every Friday when we meet together for family time will be Fun Friday. We might do a craft or an activity or play a game—something fun to help us learn more about the week's very important subject.

What better way to kick things off than with a dance? We can wiggle and jiggle and do our dance together. First, let's choose a song we all enjoy. When we turn on the music, each person should start dancing in a way that reflects what it means to love. Can you do that?

(When dancing time is over, talk about the activity using the following questions.)

Did you have fun dancing? Whose dance made you laugh the most? Whose dance reflected love the most? Does love make us feel happy enough to dance? Why or why not?

Loving others is such a wonderful purpose for our lives. It makes the world go round. It motivates us to open the door for someone else instead of rushing right through. It pushes us to get Mom a drink of water instead of always asking her for one. Love even encourages us to let our friends or family members play with our favorite toys.

God loves love, and He wants us to be a reflection of His love to everyone we meet. Do you think you can do that?

Let's finish up with one more fun activity: a charade game of love. One of us will take a turn acting out something we can do to show love to someone in our lives. The rest of us will try to guess what that is. Go ahead, pick the most outrageous thing you can. Love knows no limits. Love big! Love always! Love well!

RESPECT

SCRIPTURE READING: EXODUS 20:12

If the president of the United States showed up at our door, would you look at him—or her—and say, "Waz up?" I doubt it. That's because certain positions demand a high level of respect. But God says we're to respect all people, no matter what their position in life.

God wants us to treat family members as nicely as we would treat the president. Why? Because each of us has been made in the image of God. We read in Genesis 1:27 that "God created man in His own image; He created him in the image of God; He created them male and female." *(Take a few minutes to memorize this verse as a family.)*

Since we're made in God's image, each of us has a great and special value. We're God's children, and He loves us a whole lot.

Do you have a favorite toy or stuffed animal you love? How would you feel if someone grabbed it and banged it on the couch? Or what if that person left it outdoors, and it got rained on? Would that make you sad? *(Explain that God may feel something like that when we show disrespect or dishonor to His other children. He doesn't like us to hurt anyone.)*

As we learn more about respect this week, look for ways to let the people in your life know you respect them. It's okay to say, "Yes, ma'am" and "Yes, sir." It's also good to look people in the eyes when they're talking to you and to use complete sentences when responding to them. Try not to answer with "Huh?" or a grunt that can't be understood.

Respect shows value. It shows that you care about the other person just as you want that person to care about you.

RESPECT

SCRIPTURE READING: MATTHEW 7:12

The more you value something, the better you treat it. But the less you value something, the worse you treat it. Respect and honor have everything to do with the value you place on a thing or person.

For today's activity, each of us will get to name two valuable things and explain how we treat those things.

(When everyone has shared, ask the following questions.)

What value do you place on God and family? How do you treat God and family? How does that compare with the way you treat your things?

To respect or honor something means to treat it as if you really like it. Let's dig deeper into this idea by talking about our toys and possessions.

- What toys or other possessions do you like the most? How do you treat them?
- Do you love God? How do you think you should treat Him?
- Do you love the members of our family? How do you think you should treat the people you love?

(Use this exercise to recognize the value each of you truly places on God and those you love most.)

RESPECT

SCRIPTURE READING: ROMANS 12:10

Examples of respect and honor can be seen in different Bible stories, including the story of Elisha in 2 Kings 2:23. We read, "[Elisha] went up from [Jericho] to Bethel; and as he was going up by the way, young lads came out from the city and mocked him and said to him, 'Go up, you baldhead; go up, you baldhead!'" (NASB).

Suddenly two bears came out of the woods and put an end to the bullying.

Respect is very important to God. And it should be to us as well. Here are some more things God says about respect:

Honor your father and your mother, that your days may be prolonged in the land which the LORD your God gives you.
EXODUS 20:12, NASB

He who mocks the poor taunts his Maker; he who rejoices at calamity will not go unpunished. PROVERBS 17:5, NASB

With [the tongue] we bless our Lord and Father, and with it we curse men, who have been made in the likeness of God; from the same mouth come both blessing and cursing. My brethren, these things ought not to be this way. JAMES 3:9–10, NASB

Honor all people, love the brotherhood, fear God. 1 PETER 2:17, NASB

In what ways can you show respect for us as parents? In what ways have you ever shown disrespect for us? Perhaps complaining when we've asked you to stop playing and get ready for bed? Or maybe pouting when it's been your turn to do a chore?

God wants us to always honor others, and He notices when we're not showing respect. So let's pay attention to how we treat others and try to show more respect.

RESPECT

Scripture Reading: Philippians 2:3

It's very difficult to respect others if we don't respect ourselves. The Bible instructs us to love our neighbors as we love ourselves (Matthew 22:39). That means we should love ourselves too! The Bible also tells us that our bodies are temples of the Holy Spirit (1 Corinthians 6:19). If such a precious gift as the Spirit of God lives in us, we need to take good care of ourselves!

There can be many reasons why we may not respect ourselves, but there is no sin, no offense, no shortcoming—no wrongdoing under heaven—that Jesus did not address through His death and resurrection. He wants us whole and able to respect ourselves!

The other side of loving ourselves as we love others is the "others." Jesus listed loving our neighbors as one of the top two commandments, right after loving God with all that we are.

Disrespect may surround you at school or at home, but you can set up boundaries and refuse to engage in disrespectful conversations. Being respectful doesn't mean that you avoid talking about your shortcomings or problems. But it does mean discussing things in ways that build up and encourage others.

Our culture tends to glorify disrespect in entertainment and politics. Humor is often used at the expense of someone else's dignity or self-respect. But remember, it's possible to be relevant and funny without reducing your dignity or that of others. You can lead the way.

Let's come up with some ways to make one another laugh and enjoy our time together. Remember to be respectful not only toward other family members but also in the things we're laughing about. *(Go around the room and have each family member share a joke or tell a funny story.)*

RESPECT

SCRIPTURE READING: 1 PETER 2:17

Music is a lot of fun. We all have songs we enjoy! Let's go around the room and share the names of our favorite songs.

It's easy to remember the words to our favorite songs, isn't it? What if we wrote our own songs as a family? Let's make that our Fun Friday activity as we wrap up this week learning about respect. It's true there are lots of songs in the world that disrespect other people. So let's add some good songs to the mix.

As we try to come up with our own song lyrics, contribute your own ideas and explain why respect is important in the song. You can tell how school, home, or church would be a better place than it is now if everyone showed more respect.

Let's bounce our lyric ideas off one another and let other family members know (respectfully, of course) if we like them and why. Then we'll put our song together into one or two stanzas and a chorus and set it to a catchy tune. And voilà! We've just written a song!

Next, we'll each design a bumper sticker about respect. Remember, a bumper sticker goes on the back of a car, so you won't have much room to work with or much time for the person driving by to see it. You'll have to summarize respect in a quick image or a few words. So get creative! Who knows, your bumper sticker might end up on a car someday.

PURITY

SCRIPTURE READING: MATTHEW 5:8

What would happen if you went outside right now with a spoon and scooped up a little bit of dirt and then came back inside and sprinkled some of that dirt into everyone's cup on the table? *(If you want to, encourage family members to do that right now.)* How does dirt change the way the drinks look? *(Encourage responses.)* When dirt is mixed into a drink, what used to be clear will now look dark and grimy.

This exercise is a great illustration of what we're going to talk about this week: purity. *Purity* simply means "freedom from contamination." Another way to describe it is something that's clean, free from anything that might spoil it somehow.

A pure apple is crisp and tasty. An impure apple has a worm in it and is brown and bruised.

Pure air is fresh and clean. Impure air has smog, dust, or allergens in it that make some of us cough or sneeze.

A pure heart thinks kind, loving, and positive thoughts. An impure heart focuses on selfishness, complaining, and being mean.

God wants our hearts to be pure, and He has told us how to do that in His Word. Philippians 4:8 says, "Whatever is true, whatever is honorable, whatever is right, whatever is pure, whatever is lovely, whatever is of good repute, if there is any excellence and if anything worthy of praise, dwell on these things" (NASB).

To dwell on something means to think deeply about it. God wants us to think only about those things that are right, pure, lovely, and good. When we do that, our hearts and our mouths will reflect what we think. As a result, what we say and do will also be pure.

PURITY

SCRIPTURE READING: PSALM 119:9

Purity means to be righteous, totally clean, or holy. Through the work of Jesus Christ on the cross, all those who believe have a clean slate and are considered pure in the kingdom of God. We want our lives to reflect this gift of purity that Jesus has given us.

(For today's activity, set a glass of water in the middle of the table and give the following instructions.) Each member of our family will get one random ingredient from the pantry or refrigerator to pour into the glass of water (ketchup, mustard, relish, etc.). Then each of us will take a turn pouring a little bit of our ingredient into the glass of water and stirring with a spoon. *(As the ingredients are added, the water becomes less pure and less drinkable. The goal of this exercise is to talk about the things family members may be pouring into their lives that don't reflect the purity we've been given in Jesus Christ. After the activity, discuss the following.)*

This week we're talking about purity. Purity means to be clean. Everyone wants to drink clean water, but when we poured different ingredients into the water, the glass of water became something we no longer wanted to drink.

Who would like to drink this whole glass of water right now?

God made us pure when we accepted Jesus Christ as savior. Now God wants to use us for great things, but we must be careful not to add things to our lives that would make Him not want to use us.

PURITY

SCRIPTURE READING: 1 TIMOTHY 4:12

God tells us in His Word that when we live our lives with pure hearts, we'll get to see Him in ways many other people won't. In Matthew 5:8 we read, "The pure in heart are blessed, for they will see God." Isn't that a great reason to live our lives with pure hearts? Let's discover what else God says about purity.

Let no one look down on your youthfulness, but rather in speech, conduct, love, faith and purity, show yourself an example of those who believe. 1 TIMOTHY 4:12, NASB

Isn't that great news? No one is ever supposed to look down on you because you're young. Instead, God wants you to show other people (yes, even older people) what it looks like to be a young person who lives with love and purity. What is one way you can show that?

How can a young man keep his way pure? By keeping it according to Your word. PSALM 119:9, NASB

How does God tell us in this verse to keep our way pure?

Pray for us, for we are sure that we have a good conscience, desiring to conduct ourselves honorably in all things. HEBREWS 13:18, NASB

What does it mean to have a "good conscience"?

Draw near to God and He will draw near to you. Cleanse your hands . . . and purify your hearts. JAMES 4:8, NASB

If you have an unkind thought in your mind or an unkind feeling in your heart, what is a good way to get rid of it?

Let's all come up with some examples of replacing an unkind thought or feeling with a pure one.

PURITY

Scripture Reading: Psalm 51:10

A seventeen-year-old young man and his father went to a restaurant for a serious conversation about purity. The father wanted his son to understand God's expectations as the son was about to leave home to attend college. The father explained to the son that God had saved him, and he could gain access to a world of purity if he used the right key. But if the son used the wrong keys, instead of entering a world of purity, he would enter a world of impurity and immorality.

After talking about purity, the father pulled out a little gray box and slid it across the table. The son opened the box and saw a gold necklace with a key-shaped charm attached. The young man said, "Dad, this necklace looks like it's for a girl. Do you really want me to wear this?"

The father kindly responded that the necklace *was* for a girl—the girl that God had planned for his son to marry one day. Then the father explained that keys allow us to open things, but not everything. Each key is cut for a specific lock. He ended the lunch by telling his son, "Take this key and only use it to access purity."

Jesus Christ wants you to access His world of purity with the key He has given you. That key is purity, and it fits only one door. To experience purity, you must place the right key in the right lock and unlock the right door.

Take a sheet of paper and some crayons, markers, or colored pencils—or use a design app on your smartphone or tablet—and draw a key to represent what you want to give the person you'll marry one day. Remember, the key isn't for you. It's for the person in your future, the one who will one day be your husband or wife.

PURITY

SCRIPTURE READING: HEBREWS 13:18

The book of Proverbs tells us, "Even a young man is known by his actions—if his behavior is pure and upright" (20:11). Purity isn't just a grown-up thing. God is very interested in your heart right now. He wants you to live a life that's pleasing to Him in every way—in what you think, say, and do.

Let's do a Fun Friday activity that illustrates how hard it can be to stay pure. We'll all crumple pieces of paper into balls. then half of us will stand on one side of the room with half the crumpled papers, and half of us will stand on the other side with the other half.

When I say "Go!" everyone throw your crumpled paper to the other side of the room. When a crumpled piece of paper lands on your side, pick it up and throw it back. We'll do this for sixty seconds.

(When the time's up, explain the following.) Did you notice how difficult it was to finish this game without any crumpled balls on your side? As soon as you threw one ball to the other side, another came right back at you. These crumpled balls represent impure and unkind thoughts, words, and actions in our lives. You might be able to overcome one temptation and throw that ball to the other side, but another temptation will often pop up.

Remember, purity in our hearts, words, and actions is an ongoing process that we need to stay on top of every day. It's not like a light switch we can just turn on and then walk away from and forget.

Let's close in prayer, asking God to help us keep our minds and hearts alert so we can remain pure.

SALVATION

SCRIPTURE READING: TITUS 3:5

Imagine you're standing in California at the edge of the ocean. The waves are splashing and tickling your toes. A cool breeze is blowing. Kids are building sand castles.

Now imagine that you're going to jump into the ocean and swim all the way from California to Hawaii. That's a very long way! Pretend to jump into the ocean right now and start swimming.

How long do you think you'll need to swim? Keep moving those arms and kicking those legs! You only have to do this for a few more months! Do you think you can get there eventually? Why or why not?

This illustration helps us understand a very big concept: our salvation. The Bible tells us that none of us are completely righteous or without sin (Romans 3:10). It also tells us that "all have sinned and fall short of the glory of God" (verse 23). We've all fallen short when it comes to being perfect and without sin, just as we'd all fall short if we tried to swim to Hawaii (though some of us would swim farther). Some of us may do more good things than others, but at the end of the day, none of us measure up completely.

That's why God sent His one and only perfect Son into the world, so that He could pay the penalty for our sins. Jesus is the only sacrifice who never sinned. It's only through our faith in Him that we receive salvation.

Let's say John 3:16 together: "For God so loved the world, that He gave His only begotten Son, that whoever believes in Him shall not perish, but have eternal life" (NASB).

SALVATION

Scripture Reading: Romans 10:9

This week we're learning about salvation. Here's one way to understand the idea of salvation: Picture it as falling but getting caught before you experience the consequences of the fall.

What does Romans 3:23 tell us? "All have sinned and fall short of the glory of God." *(Help family members memorize the verse.)*

The good news of salvation is that something bad has been made good. If you were to fall down, that would be bad. But if you were to fall down and someone was there to catch you, it would turn out to be a good thing.

To illustrate, let's do a trust fall. We'll need one volunteer who is willing to fall backward and trust everyone else to catch him or her. That person must turn around, with his or her back facing the family and eyes closed, and fall backward with arms crossed in front.

The rest of us will stand nearby, ready and able to catch you when you fall. We're here for you!

(When you've finished the activity, discuss how this is a picture of salvation.)

How is a trust fall like salvation? *(Allow time for discussion.)* We're all like the "faller," aren't we? We're helpless to save ourselves, but Jesus Christ loves us and will catch us when we put our trust in Him.

Let's close in prayer, thanking Jesus for His wonderful gift of salvation.

SALVATION

Scripture Reading: Ephesians 2:8–9

What does it mean to believe in Jesus Christ? It's a little like being on a boat that's sinking. You can get into the lifeboat and be saved. But it won't do you any good if you don't get in.

It's also like sitting in a chair. You might say you believe that a chair can hold your weight. But that claim is meaningless until you actually sit down. Sitting down is an act of *real* faith.

Stand up and look at the chair or couch you've been sitting on. Do you trust that it will hold you? Saying you trust it is one thing. How can you *show* you trust it? By sitting down. Go ahead and sit down.

Saying we trust Christ is one thing, but asking Him to be our Lord and savior shows we believe that He truly is.

Let's review some Bible verses on salvation:

For God so loved the world, that He gave His only begotten Son, that whoever believes in Him shall not perish, but have eternal life.
JOHN 3:16, NASB

All have sinned and fall short of the glory of God.   ROMANS 3:23

The wages of sin is death, but the gift of God is eternal life in Christ Jesus our Lord.   ROMANS 6:23

(Challenge family members to memorize all three verses. See if you can learn them right now.)

SALVATION

SCRIPTURE READING: ACTS 4:12

One day a honeybee was buzzing around a little girl at a picnic. She screamed and ran away because she was scared the bee might sting her. The bee kept buzzing around and wouldn't leave this little girl alone. Her mother saw what was happening, so she got up and snatched the bee right out of the air. After holding the bee for a few seconds, she let it go.

The bee flew back to the little girl and started buzzing around her again. The girl yelled, "Mommy, the bee is going to sting me. Why did you let it go?"

The mother replied, "That bee isn't going to sting you because it already stung me. It can only sting once. All that bee is doing now is making a lot of noise, but its sting is gone."

When Jesus Christ died on the cross, He saved us from the sting of death. Death is still buzzing around us today, but those who believe in Jesus don't have to worry about being stung. He took the stinger right out of death. After three days He let death go by rising from the grave. Now death is just making a lot of noise, but its sting is gone forever.

For today's activity, we need a volunteer to pretend that he or she is a bee. Start buzzing around another person now. Pretend you're going to sting that person but don't. Now the rest of us will chase the bee, and whoever is the first to catch the bee will get tickled, or stung. (We aren't going to let the bee really sting someone!)

Once the tickling session is over, release the bee. Its "sting" is gone, so no one needs to fear it anymore.

SALVATION

Scripture Reading: Acts 16:30-31

Do you remember imagining that you were swimming from California to Hawaii? What did that activity illustrate? What did you learn this week about salvation? Let's talk about it right now. When we're done talking, I have another Fun Friday challenge for us to try. *(Go around the room so that each person has a turn to talk about what he or she learned about salvation this week.)*

Now everybody stand up. First, let's do a little stretching. *(Encourage everyone to stretch.)* Now we're going to have a contest to see who can jump the longest. You can jump any way you choose. You can hop on both feet or use only one foot, you name it. But you can't *stop* jumping. As soon as you stop, you're out of the contest. When I say "Go!" start jumping.

(When you have a winner, talk about the jumping contest.) "Who stopped first? Why? Who jumped the longest? Would that person be able to jump nonstop from now until next week? Even though that family member jumped for a long time today, jumping all the way until next week isn't possible.

No matter how great you are, or how great I am, none of us are perfect. We all make mistakes, and we all sin, which simply means that we fall short of God's standard of perfection. Just as none of us could jump until next week, none of us can live without sinning. Both are simply impossible.

That's why we all must come to Christ alone with faith alone for our salvation. He's the one who made the impossible possible by dying to give us eternal life. Jesus is our only way to heaven. Trusting in Him is how we're saved.

SPIRITUAL WARFARE

SCRIPTURE READING: EPHESIANS 6:12

Do you know there's an invisible war going on all around us? It's a huge war. It started at the beginning of time, and it's being fought throughout the earth, yet nobody has ever seen it. That's because it's a *spiritual* war.

What exactly is a spiritual war? Have you ever heard someone talk about *spiritual warfare*? It sounds a bit like a sci-fi movie, doesn't it? Is it real? Do you think it affects kids like you? *(Allow time for discussion.)* Yes, spiritual warfare *is* real. And it *does* affect you and me!

Spiritual warfare is the conflict between God and Satan that happens in the invisible spiritual world and plays out in the visible, physical world at the same time.

While spiritual warfare doesn't take place here on Earth in a specific country with weapons we can physically handle, it does affect us! The spiritual world really, truly exists even though we can't see it. But Satan wants to distract us from the battle that's happening in the spiritual world, so he tries to get us to focus on anything we can see, taste, touch, hear, or smell.

To emphasize this truth, let's have one person stand on a chair and hold up a napkin. *(If you don't have a napkin, you can use a tissue.)* When the person on the chair drops the napkin, the rest of us will start blowing at it.

What happened to the napkin? Did it move? What moved it?

You couldn't see your breath blowing, but it affected what happened to the napkin, didn't it? The same is true in spiritual warfare. What we can't see in the spiritual realm (angels, demons, Satan, even God) is battling to influence what's going on in the world we can see!

SPIRITUAL WARFARE

SCRIPTURE READING: 2 CORINTHIANS 10:3

This week we're learning about spiritual warfare. Spiritual warfare and Satan are invisible to our physical eyes, but they affect each of us and the world we see and hear every day.

Some of the invisible things in our world are good, and some of them are bad. When you get sick, is that good or bad? There are invisible bacteria and germs that aren't good for your body. But there are also white blood cells in your body that fight the bad bacteria so you feel better. You can't see it happening inside your body, but you know it's there by the way you feel.

To illustrate what an invisible war is really like, we'll go around the room and have each person name a different type of sickness. It can be a big sickness or small one.

Next, we'll take turns sharing what can help us get better when we're fighting sickness. *(After everyone has had a chance to share, continue the discussion as follows.)*

Our bodies naturally have white blood cells. The job of these blood cells is to fight infections and diseases. They help get bad invaders out of our bodies. Have you ever seen white blood cells fighting an illness so you'll feel better?

The "war" inside our bodies is invisible, but we know it's happening by the way our bodies respond. Likewise, spiritual warfare is invisible, but the white blood cells of the kingdom of God are fighting against the infectious diseases of Satan's evil realm.

SPIRITUAL WARFARE

SCRIPTURE READING: DEUTERONOMY 28:7

God's Word tells us everything we need to know about spiritual warfare—including some pretty amazing pieces of clothing that help us fight Satan's sneaky schemes.

Clothes that help fight the Devil? That sounds pretty crazy, doesn't it? But think about it this way. Have you ever played a sport or done something that required special equipment to protect you and help you do your best? Football players wear helmets and pads. Swimmers wear caps and goggles. Ballerinas wear leotards and ballet slippers. It's important to match the right equipment to the right activity. You wouldn't show up for football practice wearing swim goggles and pointe shoes!

When the Enemy tries to get you to worry or think bad thoughts about yourself or make wrong choices, you can put on God's special clothes—His armor—and stand strong. Let's find out more about God's armor by reading Ephesians 6:14–17:

> *Stand firm therefore, having [1] girded your loins with truth, and having [2] put on the breastplate of righteousness, and having [3] shod your feet with the preparation of the gospel of peace; in addition to all, [4] taking up the shield of faith with which you will be able to extinguish all the flaming arrows of the evil one. And [5] take the helmet of salvation, and [6] the sword of the Spirit, which is the word of God. (NASB)*

How many pieces of armor has God given you to fight with? *(Six.)* Now describe each one. *(Girding our loins with truth, putting on the breastplate of righteousness, shodding our feet with the preparation of the gospel of peace, and taking up the shield of faith, the helmet of salvation, and the sword of the Spirit.)*

Now that we've read about God's armor, let's talk about what it means to put on each piece. Be sure to give a specific example of how each one can help you fight against Satan's schemes.

SPIRITUAL WARFARE

SCRIPTURE READING: MATTHEW 18:18–20

L aser tag is fun! A group of friends meet in a special room, put on their vests, and grab their laser weapons.

These weapons send invisible signals to the opposing team's vests. When the blue team zaps the red team, or the red team zaps the blue team, they can't see the lasers shooting "bullets," but they feel the vibrations of the vests when they're hit.

In laser tag, invisible bullets fly all over the room. Your job isn't to run from the lasers but to recognize who is shooting them. If a shooter has on a vest that's the same color as yours, you know those invisible bullets aren't directed at you. But if someone wearing a different color vest is shooting at you, you can expect to feel the "hit" as a physical vibration.

Spiritual warfare is a lot like laser tag. There are two teams at war: God's team and Satan's team. God is shooting grace, mercy, love, and life our direction. But Satan is shooting anger, depression, guilt, shame, and death. We can't see these bullets coming because both teams are invisible. Yet even though we can't see them, we can definitely feel when we've been hit.

The secret to winning laser tag is to stay close to your team, because when you see the Enemy coming, you can all fire together, and the other team won't know what hit it.

Let's play a pretend game of laser tag right now! We'll pick teams and aim our lasers at our opponents. You'll have to rely on everyone being honest in this game. If your laser hits someone, yell out "Hit" and fill in the person's name. After three hits, that person is out. The last team standing with at least one player wins!

SPIRITUAL WARFARE

SCRIPTURE READING: PSALM 91:1–6

Spiritual warfare is taking place all around us. The battle involves angels and demons and our own sinful hearts. But God has given us everything we need to be champions in this war. This week we talked about the armor of God. For today's Fun Friday activity, we're going to make a model of God's armor. Here are some options:

1. We can get out some old magazines and look for pictures that show different pieces of "armor." For example, a picture of shoes can be the "shoes of peace." Cut out each picture you find that represents the armor. Draw yourself on a blank piece of paper and then paste the different pictures onto the paper.

2. We can find old cardboard boxes and/or brown paper bags and use them to make the different pieces of the armor of God. Work with other family members to create all six pieces of armor.

3. Or we can act out a spiritual-warfare drama. One person will play the evil Devil tempting another family member to do something wrong (like cheating on a test or copying home-work answers). The person being tempted will choose a piece of God's armor to defend against this attack. Act out the drama several times using different pieces of armor.

Enjoy this activity, but remember, spiritual warfare is a real battle. It should never be taken lightly. The first thing you should do when facing this challenge is pray. Prayer is the key to using all the pieces of armor well. The apostle Paul tells us, "With all prayer and petition pray at all times in the Spirit, and with this in view, be on the alert with all perseverance and petition for all the saints" (Ephesians 6:18, NASB).

SPIRITUAL GROWTH

SCRIPTURE READING: COLOSSIANS 1:10

(Round up some baby pictures of your family members beforehand to show or pass around during your time together.)

To illustrate this week's topic, I found some old baby pictures to pass around. Let's look at the babies in these pictures. Do you recognize any of them? What happens to little babies over time? *(Encourage responses.)*

All babies grow, just as you and I have grown. No baby stays small forever. Can you imagine what this world would be like if every baby stayed a baby? That would be a funny world, wouldn't it?

What things wouldn't happen if everyone was a baby? Let's try to imagine that right now.

How would sporting events be different if every player was a baby?

Try to imagine your teacher at school as a baby. How would that affect what happened in the classroom?

It's important to grow, isn't it? Just as it's important to grow physically, God wants us to experience *spiritual growth*. God doesn't want any of us to stay babies spiritually forever. He wants us to learn how to study His Word and understand it, listen to what He is saying, develop stronger patience muscles, and grow in our ability to love others! He wants us to mature and grow up on the inside as well as the outside!

Let's look again at these pictures of our family members as little babies. How has each family member changed compared with the way he or she was back then? What's the difference between being a spiritual baby and being spiritually mature, or grown up?

(Close in prayer, thanking God for helping each family member continue to grow in Him.)

SPIRITUAL GROWTH

SCRIPTURE READING: 2 PETER 3:18

This week we're learning about spiritual growth. Just as you get bigger and taller as you get older, your spirit also grows as you get older in your relationship with Jesus. We all start out as babies and grow to become adults—both outside and inside.

What are some things you must do to get physically bigger and stronger and eventually become a full-grown adult? What are some things you must do to become bigger and stronger as a Christian? *(Answers might include studying the Bible, praying, trusting God, and being obedient to God.)*

Spiritual growth is the process by which a believer goes from being an infant in the faith to being spiritually mature. People who become Christians are "born again." However, even though their faith in Christ brings them into God's kingdom, their experience of that kingdom grows as they grow spiritually over time.

Let's talk about when you were born . . .

(For today's activity, be ready to tell some stories about your children when they were very young. Talk about the day and time they were born. Describe what they were able to do for themselves in various stages of infancy. Ask how much your children can remember about being infants. Ask what they remember about you, their parent, when they were babies.)

Just as a baby is born into this world at a specific time, there's a specific time when a person believes in Christ and is born into a new spiritual life. Each baby born into this world is created to grow up. Likewise, a spiritual infant wouldn't be healthy if he or she remained an infant forever. It's important that each of us grows up in our faith, leaving infancy behind and becoming spiritually mature so that we can know God better and fully experience the life He has for us.

SPIRITUAL GROWTH

Scripture Reading: Hebrews 6:1–2

Growing spiritually is a lot like growing physically. You need to feed yourself to grow physically, right? You also need to feed yourself to grow spiritually. What does it mean to feed yourself spiritually? *(Encourage responses.)* We get spiritual food by spending time in God's Word, praying, and hearing about God's truths in church.

Let's look at some Bible verses to better understand spiritual growth:

Speaking the truth in love, let us grow in every way into Him who is the head—Christ. Ephesians 4:15

God says to speak both truth and love. How does love affect what we say? Can you give an example?

May the Lord cause you to increase and abound in love for one another, and for all people, just as we also do for you. 1 Thessalonians 3:12, NASB

Growing spiritually means having so much love in us that it overflows to others. Talk about someone you know who overflows with love. How can you tell?

Leaving the elementary teaching about the Christ, let us press on to maturity. Hebrews 6:1, NASB

Maturity means making wise decisions and not just decisions that feel good. Can you name a time when you made a wise decision, but it wasn't what you truly wanted?

Like newborn babies, long for the pure milk of the word, so that by it you may grow in respect to salvation. 1 Peter 2:2, NASB

How often does a baby need to drink milk? How often do we need to think about God to grow spiritually? What are some ways you can think about Him every day?

Jesus increased in wisdom and stature, and in favor with God and with people. Luke 2:52

What happened when Jesus grew spiritually "in wisdom and stature"? What is favor?

SPIRITUAL GROWTH

SCRIPTURE READING: EPHESIANS 4:15

Do you like to garden? Do you like to get your hands in the dirt and dig? That's a lot of what gardening is. It's about preparing the soil to plant a seed. When you see flowers or food growing from the ground, it's because several things were present to encourage that growth.

The first thing needed for something to grow in the ground is soil. Plants, flowers, and food need good soil to start growing. Just as plants need this foundation, we as Christians need a good foundation to grow spiritually. Jesus is our foundation. And just as a seed needs to rest in the ground, we need to rest in Jesus. *(Look up John 15:4 and read it aloud.)*

Jesus gives us what we need to "bear fruit" in our lives. Bearing fruit means to produce those things that reflect God—things like love, peace, kindness, goodness, gentleness, and self-control (Galatians 5:22–23).

Guess what else is needed for plants, flowers, and food to grow? *(Encourage responses.)* All plants need sunshine! Light helps give the plants what they need to grow. You and I need light too. Let's think about what that light might be. Can you guess? *(Allow time for discussion.)*

(Look up Psalm 119:105 and read it aloud.) What does God give us as light to help us grow spiritually? Yes, it's God's Word.

We need to stay connected with Jesus and also spend time in God's Word. When we do these two things, we'll grow spiritually. Before we finish our time together, let's go outside and plant something. Digging in the soil will remind us how important a good foundation is for living things to grow!

SPIRITUAL GROWTH

SCRIPTURE READING: 1 TIMOTHY 4:15

Growth happens all around us. Have you ever seen a puppy growing into a dog? Or a flower bud growing into a bloom? Or a tree slowly growing taller and putting out leaves? Spiritual growth looks different from these things, but we can still see it in many ways.

When you grow spiritually, you make better choices. You have better responses when someone upsets you. You're kinder and gentler, and you smile more. This is because you're letting your heart and mind line up with God's heart and mind.

For this week's Fun Friday activity, each of us will make a poster of a growing tree. First, we'll cut out some paper in the shape of a tree trunk and color it brown. Then we'll paste it onto another piece of paper. We'll also need to cut out green paper for grass or color the paper green. Be sure to put branches on your tree trunk! And put a bright yellow sun in the sky, because we all need light to grow. Plants and trees need sunlight. And we, as people, need Jesus' light.

Next, we'll collect leaves from trees outside and glue them onto our spiritual-growth posters. Let's pick lots of different types of leaves to remind ourselves that growing spiritually happens in different areas of our lives.

Sometimes growing spiritually means having the courage to speak up and say something true that might not be easy to say. At other times, growing spiritually means having the wisdom to keep our mouths closed (especially if you feel like talking back to us or your teacher)! So choose many different leaves to decorate your tree. We'll hang up the posters here at home as reminders that we need to grow spiritually.

FAITH

SCRIPTURE READING: HEBREWS 11:1

What is faith? It's an action! Faith involves more than our feelings; it involves our feet. We're to walk by faith, not just talk by faith. Faith means actually *doing* something, not just *feeling* something. Can you think of an example of what that looks like? *(Encourage responses.)*

The African impala is an animal that looks like a deer. Other African animals, such as the lion, leopard, and cheetah, consider the impala a tasty dinner treat!

But the impala has a special ability to defend itself. It can leap as far as thirty feet and as high as ten feet. Now imagine an impala playing basketball! Game over, right?

Even though the impala can leap so far and jump so high, it can easily be kept in a zoo enclosure with a fence that's only three feet high. (That's just a little higher than an average dinner table.) Why do you think that is? Because the impala won't jump over a fence if it can't see where its feet will land. An impala doesn't have faith.

You may have heard someone talk about taking "a leap of faith." God made the impala able to leap, but it won't unless it can see where it's going to land. You are made in the image of God (Genesis 1:27), and just like the impala, you've been given great gifts and abilities. God also has a plan for you—and it isn't to be eaten by a lion! Can you trust God to provide a landing place for you when you take a leap of faith? Faith means doing what God says even if you can't see where that might take you.

Let's pray together and thank God for His gift of faith.

FAITH

SCRIPTURE READING: ROMANS 10:17

Together let's learn and practice a definition of *faith* that we can recite anytime: Faith is acting like something is so, even when it's not so, that it might be so simply because God said so. That's a bit of a tongue twister, isn't it? *(Repeat the definition aloud together until everyone has it memorized.)*

Faith is acting like God is telling the truth. It's doing what God's Word says to do, even if you feel like doing it a different way, or even if you don't understand.

Do you always want to do what we tell you to do? Do you always understand everything we ask you to do?

Faith is doing what we ask of you, even if you don't understand or want to do it, because you know that we love you and want the best for you.

For today's activity, we need one volunteer who is willing to demonstrate faith. That person will walk to a designated place in the house to retrieve a designated object and bring it back to the table. Here's the catch! The volunteer must do it all with eyes closed and ears open, listening only to the voice of the person who is giving directions.

The goal of this activity is to walk by the words you hear and not by the things you see. This is an example of the Christian life. We can't see God, but we have His Word, and He expects us to act on it.

FAITH

SCRIPTURE READING: MARK 11:22–24

God loves faith. Why? Because faith shows that we believe Him. Don't you like it when someone believes you? None of us like it when we tell someone the truth, but that person doubts us. But when someone trusts us, we're glad. What about you?
Let's see what God says about faith in His Word.

The Lord said, "If you had faith like a mustard seed, you would say to this mulberry tree, 'Be uprooted and be planted in the sea'; and it would obey you." LUKE 17:6, NASB

We walk by faith, not by sight. 2 CORINTHIANS 5:7

Faith is the assurance of things hoped for, the conviction of things not seen. HEBREWS 11:1, NASB

Without faith it is impossible to please [God], for he who comes to God must believe that He is and that He is a rewarder of those who seek Him. HEBREWS 11:6, NASB

Let's each take a pen or pencil and draw a dot on a piece of paper— just a normal dot like one you'd see at the end of a sentence. Now look at each person's dot. It should be about the size of a poppy seed or a mustard seed. Those are really tiny seeds! And God says that's all the faith we need to do really great things.

Pure faith is powerful, even in small sizes!

FAITH

Scripture Reading: Ephesians 2:8–9

A little boy was upstairs in his bedroom listening to music. Suddenly he heard screams coming from outside his window. When he opened it, he heard someone yell, "Hey, the building is on fire! You have to jump out of your window!"

The boy was struck with fear. He was scared because the building was on fire, but he was also scared to jump out of the window.

He heard the voice again. "The building is on fire! You have to jump!" But the boy didn't jump, and the people outside couldn't understand why he wouldn't save himself. They didn't know he was blind and couldn't see where he was jumping.

Then the boy heard a voice call out, "Danny, jump!" Once he heard that voice, he quickly jumped out of the window and landed in the arms of his father. When he heard his father's voice, he had the confidence to jump even though he couldn't see.

Faith means being willing to do what God says when we hear His voice, even if we can't see where we're going or how we'll get there.

(To illustrate the point, ask for a volunteer for the following activity. If your child is too heavy to pick up, skip the first activity.) Close your eyes right now. I'm going to pick you up. Keep your eyes closed. How do you feel? Does it feel scary to be picked up with your eyes closed? No peeking.

Now try taking a few steps with your eyes closed. It throws things off balance, doesn't it?

Walking by faith is sometimes like walking with your eyes closed, because you don't know what's going to happen. But God does. He sees everything, so when you have faith in Him, you can trust Him to guide you, hold you, and be with you at all times.

FAITH

SCRIPTURE READING: MATTHEW 21:21–22

Raise your hand if you believed that you were going to have dinner tonight. Did we all raise our hands? Without realizing it, each of us had faith today. We believed in something we couldn't see.

We have faith all the time. We have faith that a chair is going to support us when we sit in it. If we didn't, we would be nervous when we sat down. Faith affects much of what we do. But God wants us to have faith in Him and what He has said in His Word. When we make decisions based on faith in Him, we get to see God act in ways we never dreamed of.

Today's Fun Friday activity is going to help us remember the importance of living a life of faith.

(Before your time together, find a rag or towel or something else to use as a blindfold.) Let's take the chairs from around the table and put them in the middle of the room. Who would like to volunteer to be blindfolded? Now we need someone to safely lead the blindfolded person through the maze of chairs to the other side of the room. You can lead using your hands and your words.

(Do this activity several times with everyone in the family.) This activity is a good illustration of the way God guides us through life. Sometimes there are obstacles and challenges we don't know about and can't see. But when we're sensitive to God's touch and His voice, He'll guide us safely through the maze of life to our final destination.

God has a great plan for you, and He wants you to get there by following Him in faith.

Let's pray together, asking God to help us trust Him more each day.

PURPOSE

SCRIPTURE READING: JEREMIAH 29:11

Walk over to the refrigerator and grab something out of it. Anything. Is it cold or hot? What did you expect it to be? Why? What if you reached into the refrigerator and grabbed something hot? What would you think? You'd probably think the refrigerator was broken. Why? Because that's not how a refrigerator is supposed to work. A refrigerator is designed to make things cold.

Why am I talking about weird things happening with our refrigerator? So you can see what it looks like when something doesn't fulfill its purpose.

Did you know that God made *you* for a specific purpose? It's a unique purpose designed especially for you—just like your fingerprints are unique to you.

When you try to be like someone else, then you're acting like a broken refrigerator. The world doesn't need two of someone else; one is enough. What the world needs is *you*, living out the purpose God created you for. So be you! You're the only one who can be the best at being you. Do what you were designed to do. Explore the talents, interests, and activities you do best. Why? Because when you explore these areas, you'll find out more clearly what God designed and created you to do and be.

When you find that out, you'll discover your purpose. Your purpose is important because it's why you were created. Keep in mind that like a refrigerator, your purpose is never only about you. You exist to help others so they can benefit as well!

PURPOSE

SCRIPTURE READING: PROVERBS 16:4

(Before you begin, find a simple puzzle that the whole family can work on together. You can usually buy them at a dollar store if you don't already have one at home. Or take a picture from a magazine, glue it to cardboard, and cut it into shapes to use as a puzzle.)

Finding your purpose is about fulfilling God's divine design for your life. It means believing that God is a purposeful God, and He created you for something specific and special. If God isn't random, that means you aren't random either. You are here for a specific purpose.

Let's have some fun putting a puzzle together. *(While you're putting the puzzle together, talk about how the pieces initially appear random and hard to get into the right places. Then, as you begin to place pieces in their correct spots, talk about how each piece is specifically designed to fit in a particular place.)*

Notice how each piece is different. That's what makes the puzzle work. The overall goal in doing a puzzle is to assemble the pieces so they match the picture on the box. When each piece serves its purpose, it becomes part of the big picture.

You are unique and special, and God will use you as part of His big picture.

Let's pray together and thank Him for creating each of us the way He has.

PURPOSE

SCRIPTURE READING: ROMANS 8:28

What would you do for free? What would you do as a job even if you weren't paid to do it? What ideas and thoughts take up the most space in your mind? What excites you? These things can be called your *passions.*

Pay attention to your passions. If you could swim laps all day long, for example, maybe a career as a swim coach or a physical education teacher in a school with a swim team would be a good idea. A career based on one of your passions will likely be more fulfilling than one that isn't. A passion can keep you going when things get boring or when you face conflicts and struggles.

First Corinthians 10:31 reminds us that our purpose is important, but whatever we do should be done for God's glory. Let's read this verse aloud together: "Whether, then, you eat or drink or whatever you do, do all to the glory of God" (NASB).

Now let's talk about skills. What are you good at? What do people compliment you on accomplishing?

If you're skilled with numbers, you might go after a degree in engineering or accounting. Or maybe you have the skill of comforting people, which could point you toward counseling or serving in a church. Focus on careers where your skills and your passions intersect. Together, your passions and your skills help form your purpose in life.

Ephesians 2:10 tells us that "we are [God's] workmanship, created in Christ Jesus for good works, which God prepared beforehand so that we would walk in them" (NASB). Let's spend some time memorizing this verse together.

PURPOSE

SCRIPTURE READING: PSALM 138:8

Everything is made for a purpose. The purpose of a refrigerator is to cool food, and the purpose of a stove is to cook food. The purpose of a microwave is to heat food, and a freezer's purpose is to freeze food. What would happen if the refrigerator decided it wanted to cook food, or the stove decided it wanted to cool food? What if the microwave decided it wanted to freeze food, and the freezer decided it wanted to heat food?

There would be a big problem! If these appliances tried to operate outside the purposes for which they were created, no one would be able to eat, and all the food would be wasted. For people to eat and not go hungry, the refrigerator, the stove, the microwave, and the freezer have to serve the purposes for which they were made.

Likewise, God created you for a specific purpose. Your creator has given you talents, gifts, and skills to do something in this world that He created you to do. The problem is, a lot of people are trying to do what everyone else thinks they should do, instead of asking their creator what He created them to do.

Just as food can be wasted if the appliances aren't doing what they're supposed to do, our lives can be wasted if we aren't doing what we were created to do. It's important to focus on and pray about what God's purposes are for your life. What does He want you to do? *(Encourage responses.)*

Let's close in prayer, thanking God for His purposes for each of us.

PURPOSE

SCRIPTURE READING: COLOSSIANS 1:16

(Before you begin, plan a simple dessert your family can make together. It can be as simple as instant pudding.)

It's been fun learning about purpose this week, hasn't it? Purpose has so much to do with why we're here and what we're going to do with our lives. When we're living out our purpose, we get into a "flow." This is when things seem to move smoothly, and when challenges do come up, we're better able to deal with them.

Another benefit of purpose is that we often don't feel like we're working hard when we are working hard. Let me give you an example. Do you have a favorite sport? Or a favorite class at school? Think of that right now. Now think about how you feel when you're working on homework for that class or practicing for that sport compared to when you're working on other things. Is there a difference? I bet there is. When you're living out your purpose in life, you enjoy what you're doing, and it comes naturally to you.

For today's Fun Friday activity, let's make a simple dessert together. *(As you make the dessert, talk about each ingredient you're using. What would happen if the milk decided to taste like salsa? Or if the instant pudding powder decided to be like laundry detergent?)*

While you're enjoying our dessert, think about how important it is to be the very special person God has created you to be. God has given you unique gifts, personality traits, interests, and experiences. He did this on purpose so you'll glorify Him and bring good to others in the unique way that only you can!

SELF-CONTROL

SCRIPTURE READING: PROVERBS 25:28

In 1947, Jackie Robinson forever changed the landscape of baseball and our country by becoming the first black Major League Baseball player. To give you some history, this was *seven years* before black students first started attending public schools with white students.

Jackie's talent and unselfish style helped him win the hearts of his teammates and fans. However, one of the most important traits Jackie displayed during his time with the Brooklyn Dodgers was his self-control. Racism was his greatest threat, not his opponents on the field. More than his great skills as a ballplayer, more than his team spirit, more than anything else, his self-control was his greatest tool. When people bullied him because of his skin color, he didn't fight back with his fists. He fought back through self-control and by playing so hard and so well, it made the bullies look foolish.

Life will challenge you, and it might not be because of your skin color. Thankfully our country has come a long way in that area. But when something unfair happens to you, how you respond is extremely important. Self-control will help you respond wisely rather than emotionally.

Let's pretend that someone just said something unfair or mean to you. How would you respond? *(Encourage discussion.)* Now answer that question in a little different way: How *should* you respond in a situation like this?

Let's do some role playing to help us get used to responding with self-control instead of reacting with hurt emotions. *(Role playing is just a game of Let's Pretend. Take turns as one family member plays the part of the bully, and the other person responds with self-control.)*

41

SELF-CONTROL

SCRIPTURE READING: TITUS 1:8

This week we're learning about self-control. As each of us grows in self-control, we discover how to do the right thing all the time, even when those around us are doing the wrong thing. God's Word is right, and it's our job as Christians to follow His guidance as we live our lives.

What do you want to be when you grow up? What do you think you have to do to get there? What kinds of bumps in the road and obstacles might come up on your journey to reach a dream or goal? *(Encourage each family member to share.)*

It takes self-control to make your dreams come true. It also takes discipline and self-control to learn and follow God's Word. But as you grow in your faith, you'll more fully experience His truth in your life.

Self-control is the ability to walk a straight line in life while traveling on an uneven road. The truth of God's Word is the straight line, and the world we live in is the uneven road. Walking on the straight line of God's Word is difficult in this uneven world. That's why we must practice self-control consistently, learning how to prevent the world from pushing us off the line of truth.

Let's close in prayer, thanking God for His gift of self-control and asking Him to help us learn to be more self-controlled each day.

SELF-CONTROL

SCRIPTURE READING: 1 PETER 4:7

Another word for self-control is *willpower*, which means "the ability to control yourself." It also means "a strong determination that enables you to do something difficult."

We sometimes say a person with self-control has composure. When you're composed, you're calm, especially in your thoughts and actions. *Restraint* is another word you might hear when someone is talking about self-control. Restraint means having control over your emotions and behavior.

The Bible has a lot to say about self-control because it's an important part of living life with wisdom. Let's look at some of those verses:

> *A man who does not control his temper is like a city whose wall is broken down.* PROVERBS 25:28

> *Every athlete exercises self-control in all things. They do it to receive a perishable wreath, but we an imperishable.*
> 1 CORINTHIANS 9:25, ESV

> *God gave us a spirit not of fear but of power and love and self-control.*
> 2 TIMOTHY 1:7, ESV

Based on these verses, why is self-control such an important quality to have? Can you describe a situation where you, or someone you know, didn't have self-control? Maybe it was a time you ate too many brownies and then paid for it with a stomachache. Or it could be a time when you said unkind things to a friend and then later felt bad because you realized you hurt his or her feelings. What would have been different if you had used self-control? (Encourage everyone to share a story.)

How can showing self-control make your life, and the lives of those around you, better?

SELF-CONTROL

SCRIPTURE READING: 2 TIMOTHY 1:7

If you ever take time to watch the gymnasts during the Olympic Games, you'll see some of the greatest athletes in the world. These young men and women have an incredible ability to jump, run, flip, and display remarkable control over their bodies. During the Olympic Games, judges score them not only on their athleticism but also on their self-control. No matter how athletic they are, they understand that they must do everything with perfect form and self-control to get good scores.

A female gymnast's flips on the balance beam are useless if she doesn't have the control to stay on the beam. A male gymnast's strength on the rings doesn't matter if he doesn't display the self-control necessary to maintain balance. Gymnasts must display their talents while exercising total self-control at the same time. Athletic talent is important for an Olympic gymnast, but talent without self-control will result in low scores.

God has given each of us gifts and talents to accomplish great things in life. However, not everyone has the self-control to make the most of those abilities. If everyone has talent, what separates those who are successful from those aren't? Our God-given talents will provide us with opportunities, but self-control will give those talents the edge.

Let's practice self-control by walking on our tiptoes all the way across the room. I know you'll be tempted to walk on the soles of your feet. It's hard to stay on your tiptoes for that long. But you can do it. It requires controlling your feet. Let's go!

SELF-CONTROL

SCRIPTURE READING: GALATIANS 5:22–23

Succeeding in life doesn't always depend on being the most talented, the biggest, or the smartest. Often, success goes to the person who is the most wise. An important part of wisdom is knowing how and when to use self-control.

For today's Fun Friday activity, let's find a place in our home or outside where we each have to walk on something thin—maybe the edge of a sidewalk or a line on the driveway. Then we'll take turns trying to walk from point A to point B without losing our balance.

You're going to discover how important self-control is when your body leans this way or that, and you have to draw on all your strength and balance to keep yourself where you want to be!

Another activity that's more challenging than fun is to see if you can go without dessert tonight. No matter how delicious the dessert appears to be, see if you can find the self-control to say, "No, thank you."

It's important to practice self-control with things like dessert. That way you'll be used to exercising self-control when harder, more tempting things come along later in life.

MONEY

SCRIPTURE READING: HEBREWS 13:5

To sow a seed, you must first let it go. You need to put the seed into the ground or the soil for it to grow. A seed actually has to die before it can bear fruit or turn into the plant, food, or flower it was made to be. Sowing is what sets the harvest in motion.

Imagine a farmer saying, "This year I'm not going to sow any seeds on my eighty acres of land. I'm trusting God for a full crop of corn because I know that He can do far more than I can ask or imagine."

Wouldn't you think that farmer had lost his mind? He can't expect his eighty acres of farmland to produce even one stalk of corn if he doesn't take the time and effort to first sow the seeds.

Yet this is what many people do with their money. They come to church or spend time with God and ask Him to bless their money without being willing to "sow"—or give God—even a little bit here or there. If we want a harvest, we have to sow seeds.

Let's practice giving to God this week. We can do that in lots of ways. It starts with a mind-set that God owns our money. What might that look like in your life? *(Encourage responses.)*

It might mean giving your snack money to a family member or friend. Or putting an offering in the offering plate or basket at church. Giving comes in many forms. When you give, you remind yourself that God is the owner of all you have, and you're planting seeds for a future harvest.

Let's close in prayer, asking God to help us learn to give generously this week.

MONEY

Scripture Reading: 1 Timothy 6:10

This week we're learning to have the right perspective on money. Why is money important? *(Encourage responses.)*

Money is important because it helps us buy the things we need, like our house, clothes, cars, and food. However, we must understand that God is the one who really provides for us. He gives us the ability to work so we can earn the money to pay for the things we need.

What special talents has God given you? One day those talents will put you in a position to make money. But it doesn't start with you. It always starts with God, and everything else comes after Him. Remember, we must keep God in His rightful place and money in its rightful place, which is under God.

How many things can you list that money can't buy? *(You might want to jot down the answers on a large sheet of paper.)* What can our mighty God do that money can't? Why is it important to keep money in the right place in our lives?

Remember, we should use our money to serve God, not the other way around. God doesn't serve money!

MONEY

SCRIPTURE READING: MATTHEW 6:24

*G*ive, *save*, *spend* are three powerful words related to money. Let's see what God's Word has to say about them.

1. *Give.* Proverbs 3:9–10 says, "Honor the LORD from your wealth and from the first of all your produce; so your barns will be filled with plenty" (NASB). God wants us to give to Him first of all. Whenever you get some money from a gift or from working, set aside some of it for God at the very start.

2. *Save.* After you set aside some of your money for God, take another portion and save it. The Bible tells us that the people of Egypt survived a seven-year famine at the time of Joseph and even fed people in other lands (Genesis 41). This happened because Joseph instructed the Egyptians to set aside— or save—a portion of every harvest during the seven years before the drought.

   Life has a way of surprising us with unexpected expenses. When we make saving money a habit, we can be better prepared for whatever happens.

3. *Spend.* Spend the rest of your money wisely. Plan your spending. Don't just spend randomly, but make sure the thing you want is truly what you want. Use self-control when you want something. Before spending your money, wait three days and then ask yourself if you still want what you were planning to buy. The Bible says in Proverbs 21:5, "The plans of the diligent lead surely to advantage, but everyone who is hasty comes surely to poverty" (NASB). There's nothing wrong with spending money or enjoying blessings in life. But use wisdom and restraint.

When you give, save, and spend, you can stop letting money be the boss that tells you what to do. Instead, as you follow God's principles, you'll watch Him bless your money.

MONEY

SCRIPTURE READING: ECCLESIASTES 5:10

One day a father took his daughter to the candy store. On the way she asked if she could hold two dollars in her hand so she could buy the candy herself. The father gave her the two dollars and held her other hand as they walked to the store. Unfortunately, it was windy outside, and the money flew out of the little girl's hand. She tried desperately to let go of her father's hand so she could chase the money. But her father wouldn't let go of her hand because he didn't want her to get hurt in the parking lot.

She yelled, "Let me go, Daddy. I have to get the money!"

The father said, "Letting go of me to chase the money can get you hurt, but if you stay with me, I can make sure you get your candy."

The confused little girl wondered how her dad was going to get her the candy. Then she watched as her father pulled a twenty-dollar bill from his pocket. The little girl quickly realized that staying with her father was more valuable than chasing the money.

God is so much more valuable than money. The problem is that most people are willing to let go of God to chase after money. But God wants to hold our hands and stay in a close relationship with us for our own good.

(Allow time for discussion after each of the following questions.)

How would you feel if your candy money went flying across the parking lot? Would you want to chase it? Or would you keep holding my hand and trust me?

Do you trust that God can provide for you even if you lose something? If this has ever happened to you, would you tell us about it right now?

MONEY

SCRIPTURE READING: MATTHEW 6:19–21

Learning to use money wisely is an important life lesson. For our Fun Friday activity, let's each make a saving and giving bank. We can make one from a jar, bowl, or cup, or even out of cardboard or envelopes.

(Have supplies ready so your family can make and decorate a bank with three compartments—one labeled "Give," another "Save," and the third labeled "Spend." You can even decorate and use envelopes.)

When someone gives you money (maybe as a gift or from doing a job), divide it among the three compartments. When it's time to spend your money, you'll know how much you have. But don't borrow from the Give and Save compartments!

Next, let's think of someone we know with a financial need and talk about how to help that person. This is a great way to discover the blessing of giving. Maybe it's a kid at school who never seems to have much for lunch. Or an elderly friend or neighbor who is struggling. *(Brainstorm ways to bless this person with the money God has given your family. It might be buying lunch for the kid at school, or even bringing some food from home.)* I know we can come up with some creative ways to bless others using the money God has blessed us with!

Here's another fun activity we can do over the weekend. Do you remember how we talked about seeds earlier this week? Let's get some seeds and plant them in a plastic cup or outside. We can water them regularly and watch them grow. This is what God can do with our money when we invest—or plant—it in the things He wants us to do, like giving to the church and giving to others!

PRAYER

SCRIPTURE READING: PHILIPPIANS 4:6

Have you ever seen a key that's attached to the outside of an envelope or a flyer you receive in the mail? Sometimes car dealerships mail out thousands of keys to lure people into their businesses. If you go to the dealership, sit in the prize car, and can start the car with your special key, you'll win a brand-new car!

But if your key doesn't start the car, you don't win anything at all. All of a sudden that key becomes useless. It's good for nothing. You might as well just throw it away.

Prayer is like a key. When it's the right key in the right car, amazing things can happen. After all, we're praying to the God who made everything! But too many people don't know how to use this key. They don't feel that prayer "works" for them, so they throw it away. Not a good idea at all. Prayer is one of the most important things we can do!

Do you want to know one of the secrets to great praying? Jesus Christ. He's the ignition the prayer key must fit in for it to work.

Let's read John 14:13 and 15:7 aloud together and then discuss some questions. *(Read both verses and allow time to discuss each question.)*

What do you have to do for your prayers to be answered?

What does it mean or look like to "abide" or "remain" in Jesus? Does that include reading your Bible? What else? Here's a hint: Abiding means to spend time with someone, as if you were living in that person's house.

PRAYER

SCRIPTURE READING: MARK 11:24

This week we're learning about the importance of prayer. Praying is simply talking to God. We can talk to God as often as we want to. He's always listening. He wants to hear about what we're thankful for and how He can help us. We don't have to be in church to pray; we just have to want to talk to God.

Let's pray together right now. As we go around the room, each of us can pray a simple prayer thanking God for something.

(Share the following prayer format and then give everyone the opportunity to pray. Encourage each family member to say his or her own prayer to God. It may feel uncomfortable if it's not something you're used to doing as a family, but you'll begin to feel more comfortable as you practice communicating with God.)

Here's how to break up your prayer into three parts:

1. Thank God for what He has done.
2. Ask God to forgive your sins and help you continue growing as a Christian each day.
3. Tell God about important needs in your life and ask for His help and guidance.

Remember, prayer is essential to building a strong relationship with God. Just as we naturally feel closer to people we communicate with often, constant communication with God through prayer brings us closer to Him. Prayer is one of the most powerful tools for Christians because it allows us to experience God's participation in our earthly lives.

PRAYER

SCRIPTURE READING: MATTHEW 6:6–7

We can pray in so many ways—and at all times. Prayer is like talking to a close friend or relative. God isn't as interested in the words we say as He is in the heart behind our words.

Are you sincere? Do you care what God thinks? Do you want to know what God wants? Ask yourself these questions when you're praying.

Here are two ways to become even better at prayer than you already are:

1. *Pray Scripture.* Pick up a Bible and start reading. Then select a verse and turn it into a prayer. Here's an example: Matthew 25:40 says, "Truly, I say to you, as you did it to one of the least of these my brothers, you did it to me" (ESV). Your prayer might be, *"God, help me reach out to the least of these in my world and treat them as Your loved children."* Or you could select a psalm as an inspiration for prayer. You could even write out the Lord's Prayer (Matthew 6:9–13) using your own words.

2. *Give thanks.* On a piece of paper or in a notebook or journal, make a list of all the things in your life or in the world that you're thankful for. If you're feeling artistic, doodle images of all the things you're thankful for today.

Now let's read what the Bible says about giving thanks.

Give thanks to the LORD, for He is good, for His lovingkindness is everlasting. PSALM 107:1, NASB

Always [give] thanks for all things in the name of our Lord Jesus Christ to God, even the Father. EPHESIANS 5:20, NASB

Give thanks in everything, for this is God's will for you in Christ Jesus. 1 THESSALONIANS 5:18

PRAYER

SCRIPTURE READING: ROMANS 8:26

When people get on an airplane, they assume the pilots are in control. However, the pilots know that to fly the plane, they must communicate regularly with the control tower. The air-traffic controllers can see everything, especially any dangers the pilots can't see. So the pilots must talk to the controllers and follow their instructions to stay safe.

God is our control tower. He's able to see things we can't see. He's able to understand things we don't understand. Our job is to rely on Him through constant communication, so He can guide us safely on the flight of life.

Prayer is the way we communicate with our control tower. It enables us to stay close to the One who is really in control. It's also the way we make our requests known to God—just as a pilot requests permission from the control tower before landing the plane.

When you order something on the Internet, do you worry that it won't arrive? Do you go back and order it again and again? Or when you order something at a restaurant, do you worry that it won't come? Do you place the same order again and again?

No, when you order something, you wait for it to come. Why? Because you're trusting and expecting it to come. The secret to living a powerful prayer life is knowing what to ask. Jesus says that if we ask anything that's in line with God's will, He'll do it (see 1 John 5:14–15). Anything! But first we need to check God's Word to see what His will is.

What kinds of things can we ask God for? A couple of examples might include asking God to give you wisdom or to reveal His purposes for your life. What other examples can you think of?

PRAYER

SCRIPTURE READING: 1 THESSALONIANS 5:17

(If your family hasn't seen the film The War Room, *you might watch it together as your Fun Friday activity. It will help you understand more about the power of prayer.)*

For our Fun Friday activity, we're going to create prayer jars. First, we'll each decorate a jar. Then at the beginning of each day, you can write a simple prayer on a rock or a piece of paper, offer your prayer to God, and then place it in your jar. Place as many prayers in your jar as you like throughout the week.

Your prayers can be whatever you feel like telling God. At the end of the week, remove the rocks or pieces of paper from your prayer jar and see how God has responded. Spend time remembering what He has done for you and thanking Him for what He's going to do for you and through you.

(If you don't want to create a prayer jar, make a prayer list or buy a journal where each family member can add his or her prayers. Then record when and how those prayers are answered. Another activity might be to spend time praying for very specific things with your family around the dinner table. Spin a globe around and then stop it. Or use a paper map or online map. Randomly point to a spot on the map or globe and then pray for that country—the people, the government, health needs, wars and civil unrest, the economy, and so on.)

You could also take a walk around your school or our home and pray specifically over these places.

Let's close in prayer together right now, thanking God for always loving us and listening to us—and for His wonderful gift of prayer!

GIVING

SCRIPTURE READING: 2 CORINTHIANS 9:7

God loves giving. In fact, He gave the greatest gift of all: His Son, Jesus Christ. John 3:16 says, "For God so loved the world, that He gave His only begotten Son, that whoever believes in Him shall not perish, but have eternal life" (NASB). God didn't keep Jesus for Himself. He didn't act selfishly. He gave.

God wants each of us to have a giving heart too. You can look for ways to make other people happy or better through your giving. You can give your time, your talents, and your money. You could give someone a kind word, a toy, or some help. There are so many ways you can give. Can you think of some other examples? *(Allow time for discussion.)*

Make sure you give from a right heart. While people might see the outside—what you say and do—God sees the reasons behind your words and actions. If you're giving to make yourself look good, or for any reason other than love and care, that doesn't honor God.

Here's what God says about the best way to give:

When you give to the poor, do not sound a trumpet before you, as the hypocrites do in the synagogues and in the streets, so that they may be honored by men. Truly I say to you, they have their reward in full. But when you give to the poor, do not let your left hand know what your right hand is doing, so that your giving will be in secret; and your Father who sees what is done in secret will reward you. MATTHEW 6:2–4, NASB

Name one way you can give something to someone else without a whole lot of people seeing or knowing about it. *(Encourage everyone to offer a response.)*

GIVING

SCRIPTURE READING: ACTS 20:35

This week we're learning about giving. Giving means taking something that's yours and giving it to someone else in need. It's more than just sharing. When you share something, you expect to get it back. When you give something, you don't expect anything in return.

We want others to feel loved just like God loves us. God loves us so much that He gave us His Son, so we should love others the same way God loves us. Giving shows the love of God in us and through us. What can you give to someone else that will make him or her feel loved?

Let's talk about ways we can become givers as individuals and as a family. Think about a person or family in need. What can we do to help? How can we express the love of God through giving?

Is it ever difficult to give? Should we let that stop us? Why is it important to give, even if it costs us something?

(After answering these questions, plan a family project that brings you together to give to a person or family in need. Encourage everyone to suggest ideas and choose the one you can do in the near future.)

Let's close in prayer, asking God to help us be cheerful givers, imitating His love for us and the way He gives so generously to us.

GIVING

SCRIPTURE READING: LUKE 6:38

Giving reflects the heart of God. There's no shortage of Bible verses on this topic, so let's dive right in!

Each person should do as he has decided in his heart—not reluctantly or out of necessity, for God loves a cheerful giver. 2 CORINTHIANS 9:7
What kind of giver does God love best? What does that look like?

In everything I showed you that by working hard in this manner you must help the weak and remember the words of the Lord Jesus, that He Himself said, "It is more blessed to give than to receive."
ACTS 20:35, NASB
Why do you think it's more blessed to give than to receive?

Give, and it will be given to you. They will pour into your lap a good measure—pressed down, shaken together, and running over. For by your standard of measure it will be measured to you in return.
LUKE 6:38, NASB
Does God give back to us when we give to others out of a pure heart?

One who is gracious to a poor man lends to the LORD, and He will repay him for his good deed. PROVERBS 19:17, NASB
There are many ways of being poor. Some people don't have enough money. Others don't have many friends, opportunity, or hope. Name a way you can be kind to the poor.

Whoever gives just a cup of cold water to one of these little ones because he is a disciple—I assure you: He will never lose his reward!
MATTHEW 10:42
Is God interested in a BIG gift as much as He is in the heart behind it? Do you consider giving someone a cup of water important? Does God?

GIVING

SCRIPTURE READING: 2 CORINTHIANS 9:6

One day at school, Danny and Jake were getting ready to pay for their lunches. When Jake reached into his pocket, he was shocked to discover that his money was gone. Danny wanted to help his friend by paying for his food, but he had only enough for himself.

Danny told Jake that he could have his lunch. At first Jake wouldn't take it, but Danny insisted. Danny was hungry, but he thought the right thing to do was to give his friend his lunch.

A short time later the school principal walked over with a bag of great-smelling food from a fast-food restaurant. The principal told Danny he saw what Danny had done and wanted to give him this special reward. Both boys had lunch because one of them was willing to sacrifice.

Giving is always a sacrifice. When we give something to someone else who is in need, we often find ourselves in a position of having to give away the very thing we need. This is why giving can be so hard. However, the Bible says it's better to give than to receive (Acts 20:35). This is because someone in heaven is watching, and He will reward us!

Let's practice giving right now. Think about something you have that someone else may want or need. It could be a special dessert or even a toy from your room. Are you willing to give it away? If you are, go ahead and do it now. You can either give it to someone in our home or talk about what you plan to give to someone else in need.

GIVING

Scripture Reading: Luke 12:33–34

Today's Fun Friday activity should kick-start a whole lot of fun! We've been learning about giving this week. Now let's brainstorm three different ways each of us can give to someone in our home this week. Write your ideas down on a large piece of paper.

But don't just write them down. Do each of these things this week! And keep in mind that the heart behind what you do is what matters most. Have a cheerful heart and open your eyes to see how God wants to bless you in return.

Another fun way to give is by affirming and encouraging others. You can affirm or encourage someone by expressing something positive about that person. It could be telling a person that he or she is a hard worker. Or it might be pointing out a specific talent you see in a family member. Maybe one of them plays the piano beautifully. Or he or she might play soccer even better. Say so!

Let's take turns right now giving words of affirmation to the person sitting to our right. We'll go around the room once, and then when we're finished, we'll reverse direction and give words of affirmation to the person sitting on our left. Get ready . . . go!

THE HOLY SPIRIT

SCRIPTURE READING: JOHN 14:26

Have you ever seen the wind? I know you've *felt* the wind, but have you ever seen it?

We can't see the wind, but we know it exists. In the same way, the Holy Spirit is real even though we can't see Him.

God's Word uses wind to describe the Holy Spirit. It says, "The wind blows where it pleases, and you hear its sound, but you don't know where it comes from or where it is going. So it is with everyone born of the Spirit" (John 3:8).

Even though we can't see the Holy Spirit, God wants us to learn how to feel His presence, hear His voice, and move when we sense His promptings in our lives. God uses the Holy Spirit to speak to us personally—to convict us of things we're doing wrong and encourage us to do the things God wants us to do.

Grab a bowl or a cup and fill it with water. Put your finger in the water. Now pull it out. What mark did your finger leave behind? Do it again and keep trying to leave a permanent mark.

Okay, you can stop. It's impossible to leave a permanent impression in water because it naturally returns to its original form.

How do you know you put your finger in the water when you see no evidence of it now?

Consider the Holy Spirit. We can't see Him with our eyes, and yet He moves among us and impacts our lives. Not being able to see Him doesn't mean He isn't there. Can you think of some examples of other things that exist even though we can't see them?

THE HOLY SPIRIT

SCRIPTURE READING: ACTS 2:38

This week we're learning about the Holy Spirit. He wants to help us live godly lives and make wise decisions. He wants us to go the right way so that we never feel lost. Anytime we don't know which way to go or what decision to make, we can pray to the Holy Spirit, and He'll help us make the right choices.

Are you in a situation right now where you don't know what to do? Let's pray that the Holy Spirit will help you make the best decision. *(Take time to pray about each situation.)*

What important decisions do we need to make as a family? Which decisions are we the most confused about? Let's write them down and pray about them together.

(Create a list on a sheet of paper of major decisions that your family needs to make. Then pray about each decision on the list and ask for the Holy Spirit's divine guidance. This activity will invite the Holy Spirit to be involved in your decisions as a family and give you the opportunity to experience His power.)

THE HOLY SPIRIT

SCRIPTURE READING: 1 CORINTHIANS 2:10

To learn about the Holy Spirit, the best place to go is to the Bible itself. Let's read and discuss what God's Word has to say about this very important member of the Trinity.

The Helper, the Holy Spirit, whom the Father will send in My [Jesus'] name, . . . will teach you all things, and bring to your remembrance all that I said to you. JOHN 14:26, NASB

What two things does the Holy Spirit do according to this verse? Have you ever experienced the Holy Spirit leading or teaching you? When?

The Spirit also helps our weakness; for we do not know how to pray as we should, but the Spirit Himself intercedes for us with groanings too deep for words. ROMANS 8:26, NASB

Did you realize the Holy Spirit prays for you? In fact, He can pray even better than you can. Sometimes it's good to tell God how you're feeling and ask the Holy Spirit to pray for you. He's ready and waiting to do just that.

The Spirit of the LORD will rest on [God's chosen king], the spirit of wisdom and understanding, the spirit of counsel and strength, the spirit of knowledge and the fear of the LORD. ISAIAH 11:2, NASB

What are some of the Holy Spirit's traits?

Hope does not disappoint, because the love of God has been poured out within our hearts through the Holy Spirit who was given to us. ROMANS 5:5, NASB

How does God pour out His love into our hearts? Did you know you can ask God to pour His love into your heart more and more each day? Sit quietly for a minute and ask the Holy Spirit to fill you up with God's love. Then be patient and wait. He'll do it.

THE HOLY SPIRIT

SCRIPTURE READING: JOHN 16:13

Sailboats depend on the wind for speed and direction. A captain sets the sail in a certain position to catch the wind so the boat will be blown in the desired direction. While there are many different types of sailboats, the wind is one thing they all rely on. Yet the wind can't be seen.

For a sailor to know the direction the wind is blowing, he must put up his sail to feel what he can't see. Even though wind is invisible, it has power over the direction of the boat. The captain has the power to set the sail, but the wind ultimately has power over the direction of the boat.

The Holy Spirit is much like the wind. You can't see Him, but you can feel His direction in your life. He has the power to lead you and "guide you into all the truth" (John 16:13). It's your job to set your sails through prayer so you're in position to hear Him. If your sails are down, you won't feel His power or influence in your life. If you want to head in the right direction, set your sails to catch the wind of the Spirit and let Him direct your life.

Let's play a quick game to illustrate this point. We'll need two volunteers. One person will pretend to be the wind while another person pretends to be the sailboat. The person playing the sailboat first needs to set the sail. You can use your arm or a stick—anything you can lift high in the air. When you're ready, the person pretending to be the wind will start blowing. Remember, whoever is the boat *must* go in the direction of the wind. You don't get to choose. Follow the wind wherever it takes you! *(After the game, point out how this illustrates the way we should follow the Holy Spirit wherever He leads us.)*

THE HOLY SPIRIT

SCRIPTURE READING: ACTS 1:8

Interacting with the Holy Spirit is often a gentle experience. Here's one example in the Bible where God spoke to the prophet Elijah through the Spirit:

> *[The Holy Spirit] said, "Go out and stand on the mountain in the*
> *LORD's presence."*
> *At that moment, the LORD passed by. A great and mighty*
> *wind was tearing at the mountains and was shattering cliffs before*
> *the LORD, but the LORD was not in the wind. After the wind there*
> *was an earthquake, but the LORD was not in the earthquake. After*
> *the earthquake there was a fire, but the LORD was not in the fire.*
> *And after the fire there was a voice, a soft whisper.* 1 KINGS 19:11–12

A soft whisper is sometimes hard to hear, isn't it? Let's try a fun experiment right now. I'll start things off and whisper a statement to the person sitting next to me. Remember, you can only use a soft whisper. That person will whisper the message to the next person, and so on.

(Once the message has been passed around the room, have the last person say it aloud.)

Now let's compare the first statement to the last. Did any of the words get jumbled up? A soft whisper isn't always the easiest thing to hear, is it?

It's very important to keep your heart, ears, and mind open to the whisper of God's Holy Spirit. You don't want to miss what He's saying to you. So pay attention and listen closely.

When you read your Bible, see if you can hear God's Spirit saying something just to you, helping you understand what you're reading. When you learn to hear the whispers of the Holy Spirit and allow Him to guide you, it will change your life and help you make wise choices.

FRIENDS

SCRIPTURE READING: JOHN 15:13

Friends are a special part of life. Having a friend gives us someone to play games with, talk to, and share fun experiences with. Being a friend gives us the opportunity to help others when they need it, to lend a listening ear, and to make them smile.

Let's talk about how to choose friends and treat our friends. Think of a friend right now and answer a couple of important questions.

Does your friend ever put you down, criticize you, or make you feel bad? If so, do you think this is what a good friend does?

Do you and your friend argue a lot and rarely come to an agreement? If that's the case, do you think he or she is a good friend to have?

A good friend is someone who takes time to learn who you are. That person also won't put you down or make you feel bad about yourself. You've been made in the image of God, so a good friend will try to point you back to God if you're having trouble in any area of your life.

It's not only important to have good friends; it's important to *be* a good friend too. That means you should learn the art of listening well.

Ask yourself, "When I talk with my friend, is it usually about myself?" What percentage of the time do you think you talk about yourself? Half the time, or more or less than that?

Friendship should be a shared experience. Sometimes you'll be there for your friend. At other times your friend will be there for you.

And always remember, there's "a friend who sticks closer than a brother" (Proverbs 18:24, NIV). That friend is Jesus Christ Himself. He's your very best friend, and He cares for you!

FRIENDS

SCRIPTURE READING: ECCLESIASTES 4:10

This week we're learning about friends. A friend is someone who is close to you and is going in the same direction you're going. It's important to make sure you have friends who want to make God happy with the way they live. Having people like these as friends will help you continue living a strong life for God. Some friends are good and some are bad.

Which of your friends love God and live for Him? Which friends don't live for God?

For today's activity, everyone will need a sheet of paper and a pen. Draw a line down the middle of your paper, creating two sections. At the top of the section on the left, write the words *Following Him*. At the top of the section on the right, write the words *Not Following Him*.

On the left side of the paper, list people in your life who live according to biblical standards. On the right side, list people in your life who don't live that way. Limit each list to ten names, and don't include family members.

(After everyone has created their lists, talk together about why it's important to have friends who reflect God's standards and help us follow Him in the best way possible.)

Let's close in prayer, thanking God for godly friends who lift us up and bring out the best in us.

FRIENDS

SCRIPTURE READING: PROVERBS 18:24

A lot goes into being a good friend and choosing good friends. Surround yourself with people who have faith in God, who love others, and who look for something positive in every situation. Let's explore what God has to say on the subject of friendship.

Iron sharpens iron, and one man sharpens another. PROVERBS 27:17
How can a good friend sharpen you to make you a better person?

Encourage one another and build each other up as you are already doing. 1 THESSALONIANS 5:11
What is one way you can encourage someone else? Has a friend ever encouraged you? What happened?

Do not be deceived: "Bad company corrupts good morals." 1 CORINTHIANS 15:33
This is a lot like peer pressure. Tell about a time you experienced peer pressure to do something you knew you shouldn't be doing.

A friend loves at all times. PROVERBS 17:17
Love is important to any friendship. Does this verse mean we're to love even when our friends annoy or ignore us? How would we show that kind of love?

Treat others the same way you want them to treat you. LUKE 6:31, NASB
The Golden Rule! What does this look like in real life?

FRIENDS

SCRIPTURE READING: JOHN 15:14–15

Peer pressure. It comes with having friends, right? What is peer pressure? *(Encourage everyone to share their ideas.)*

Keep in mind, peer pressure can be either good or bad. For example, if someone pressured you to do your homework during study hall, would that be considered good peer pressure? Or if someone was running laps at full speed during gym class and was showing respect to the teacher, would that be good or bad peer pressure? Why?

What might be an example of bad peer pressure? It could be as simple as someone at church encouraging you to pass notes during the lesson. *(Encourage each family member to give an example.)*

Now let's come up with some examples of positive peer pressure and talk about them for a minute.

Which kind of peer pressure do you think God wants you to use with your friends?

Which kinds of friends do you think God wants you to hang around—those who are modeling and encouraging mostly positive things or mostly negative things? Why?

There's an old saying, "Show me your friends, and I'll show you your future." This means that our friends often influence us whether we realize it or not. The friends we choose can have a big impact on other choices we make, which will affect our future.

Choosing friends is about much more than finding people who are fun to be around. It also has to do with hanging around those who love God and honor Him with their words and actions.

FRIENDS

SCRIPTURE READING: PROVERBS 17:17

Let's review what a good friend is and does. A good friend . . .

- can be depended on,
- remembers important things like your birthday or your accomplishments,
- uses kind words,
- does nice things for you,
- gives you help when you need it most, and
- likes to spend time with you and talk with you.

Those are things a good friend does for you. But those are also things you should do to be a good friend to someone else! Remember, *being* a good friend is just as important as *having* a good friend!

For today's Fun Friday activity, we'll role-play what it means to be a good friend. One of you will pretend you're having a bad day. Maybe you got a bad grade on a test, or someone said something about you that wasn't nice. Those are suggestions, but you can decide what turned it into a bad day.

Someone else will act out what it looks like to be a good friend in a situation like that. Are you ready? Go for it! *(Encourage participation. You might need to play a part yourself!)*

For our next role-playing activity, one of you will pretend that you're at school during recess, but you're standing by yourself and don't have anyone to play with. Another volunteer will demonstrate what it looks like to be a good friend. What can you say to help cheer the person up? What can you do?

Have fun acting out different scenarios to learn how a good friend would behave! Then in real life, always remember to be a good friend to those around you.

Let's pray that God will help each of us be the kind of friend that honors Him.

FAMILY

SCRIPTURE READING: COLOSSIANS 3:20

Family is first mentioned in the Bible in the book of Genesis. The family existed even before there was sin. The first family was placed in a sinless environment that God created.

On the fifth day of creation, God formed the animals that would live on the earth. Then on the sixth day, He came to the greatest purpose of all: creating people. Us. You and me.

In Genesis we read,

> *God created man in His own image, in the image of God He created him; male and female He created them. God blessed them; and God said to them, "Be fruitful and multiply, and fill the earth, and subdue it; and rule over the fish of the sea and over the birds of the sky and over every living thing that moves on the earth."* 1:27–28, NASB

The purpose of humankind is to reflect the image of God. An image is simply a mirror—a reflection of something or someone. We're to look so much like God that we reflect Him to others. Our families are to reflect Him as well. The purpose of a family is to be a team that God can work through to carry out His will and bring Him glory.

What is one way our family can help others know about God?

What is one way our family can reflect God and His attitudes and character to one another?

Let's think of something we can do together that will benefit our church, our neighborhood, or someone we all know. *(Discuss ideas, decide on a plan, and then carry it out.)*

FAMILY

SCRIPTURE READING: EXODUS 20:12

This week we're learning about the importance of the family. Our family is very important to God, and we want to do everything we can to make it strong.

What do you think you can do better to help us be stronger as a family?

What do you think we as parents can do better to help us be stronger? We love you, and we want to do whatever that takes. God wants us to have a strong family, so let's give it to Him!

Family is extremely important to God's plan in this world. This is why Satan seeks to tear the family apart. His plan is the exact opposite of God's plan. He wants to prevent the earth from being filled with the image of God and instead make sure it's filled with sin, which is the opposite of what God wants.

For today's activity, we'll discuss the ways we see the Enemy attacking our family to separate us. As we identify those areas, let's ask God for forgiveness if we've harmed a family member. Then we'll talk about ideas for building up our family.

(The goal of this discussion is to identify cracks in the family and seal them before the Enemy is able to do more damage. After the discussion, ask God to help where help is needed.)

FAMILY

SCRIPTURE READING: 1 TIMOTHY 3:4

God spells out pretty clearly in His Word what a family is to be like. Let's talk about the way God sees family and how He wants each of us to relate to one another.

Honor your father and your mother so that you may have a long life in the land that the LORD your God is giving you. EXODUS 20:12

Sons are indeed a heritage from the LORD, children, a reward. Like arrows in the hand of a warrior are the sons born in one's youth. Happy is the man who has filled his quiver with them. PSALM 127:3–5

Teach a youth about the way he should go; even when he is old he will not depart from it. PROVERBS 22:6

Husbands, love your wives, just as Christ loved the church and gave Himself for her. EPHESIANS 5:25

Husbands are to love their wives as their own bodies. He who loves his wife loves himself. EPHESIANS 5:28

Wives, submit yourselves to your own husbands so that, even if some disobey the Christian message, they may be won over without a message by the way their wives live. 1 PETER 3:1

God sure does have a lot to say about families, doesn't He? When we seek to follow His commands and treat one another the way He asks us to, we'll see and experience His blessings in our lives. Let's make an extra effort today and every day to live out our roles in our home the way God wants us to.

FAMILY

SCRIPTURE READING: 1 TIMOTHY 3:5

A married couple named Derek and Nicole Massie decided to adopt a child who was all alone in the world. They wanted to give that child a mom and dad, and ultimately a new home. Once they adopted their son, they gave him the name Simeon. They also gave him a room in their house, clothes to wear, and food to eat. Everything that was theirs immediately became his, too.

They took full responsibility for Simeon's life, health, strength, and well-being. Simeon no longer had to worry about who would care for him, love him, and take care of his needs. He no longer had to worry whether someone different would be there when he came home. He no longer had to worry whether he was going to eat or get a good night's sleep. Even though Simeon was still getting used to his new home and new parents, there was no doubt in his little mind that he was now a part of their family.

Adoption isn't just for children like Simeon. Those who have accepted Jesus Christ as their personal savior have been adopted into the family of Abraham. That's why we can sing the song "Father Abraham." It says, "Father Abraham had many sons. Many sons had father Abraham. I am one of them."

Because God has adopted us, we're no longer alone; we're part of the body of Christ. Because of our adoption, we no longer have to worry about being separated from God. Because of our adoption, we no longer have to try to figure out life on our own. When God adopts us, we even take on a part of His name: CHRISTian.

(If your family enjoys music, sing the "Father Abraham" song together. If you don't know it, you can listen to it online and sing along.)

Let's pray together and thank God for welcoming us into His forever family.

FAMILY

Scripture Reading: Joshua 24:15

Families come in all shapes and sizes, and no two families are exactly alike. In some families, grandparents play a big part in raising the grandkids. In others, the grandparents live far away. In some families, cousins seem like sisters or brothers. In others, there might not be any cousins at all.

No family is perfect. But every family has something to celebrate because God brought us together for a reason, and that reason is to reflect His glory in all we do and say.

For today's Fun Friday activity, we're going to draw a picture that looks like a family tree. As we do, we'll talk about the different members of our family. *(Personalize these descriptions to fit your own family.)* Let's be sure to include in our pictures every relative we can think of, including the members of our family, Grandma and Grandpa, aunts and uncles, and cousins. Draw a face to represent each one. You can put each relative on a different branch of the tree.

As you draw your family tree, mention something about each person that makes you smile. Does that person make you laugh? Does he or she understand you well? Do you love that person's hugs?

Try to think of something special about each member of our family and give an example of when you experienced it yourself. You could even think of a text message you might send to family members to encourage them or let them know you're grateful they're in our family.

(Start drawing. Start talking. Family matters!)

MANHOOD

SCRIPTURE READING: EPHESIANS 5:25–27

For the next two weeks, our family is going to see what God's Word says about the roles of men and women. Both genders should have the same opportunities to do and be what God has called them to do and be. But physical differences between males and females limit their abilities and opportunities; that's just a fact of life.

In the Bible we learn about differences in men's and women's roles, especially when it comes to marriage and the church. Though men and women have equal roles, those roles are different. It's like the Trinity: God, the Father; God, the Son; and God, the Holy Spirit. Each person in the Trinity is equal in value but different in function.

God wants boys and girls to grow into men and women who understand the roles He has given them in marriage and the church, so that each can be and do his or her best for the Lord.

(Leader, over the next two weeks, you may need to adapt the wording of some questions, content, and activities depending on the number of boys and girls in your family. Rephrase to match your own family structure as you teach God's truth about manhood and womanhood.)

What are some things that both boys and girls can do in the same way? *(Encourage responses.)* How are boys and girls different in the things they can do?

We often see examples of physical differences in the world of sports. Let's see if each of us can name at least one. *(There are separate professional teams for men and women to keep the competition fairer because of differences in physical strength. In school, there are usually separate teams for boys and for girls.)*

Since the National Football League has only men's teams, does that mean a woman could never belong in the NFL? *(No. There are women doctors on the teams, as well as female physical therapists and referees.)*

Do differences between men and women and different roles mean that one person is more valuable than the other? Why or why not?

MANHOOD

SCRIPTURE READING: 1 KINGS 2:2–4

This week we're going to focus on the role of men. The definition of *true manhood* for a Christian is "a male who learns how to listen to God and live his life in obedience to Him." To put it another way, for Christian men to truly be men, they have to be obedient to God just as children have to be obedient to their parents.

Before this talk, what did you think true manhood was about? Where did you get your ideas about true manhood? We often get our ideas from our culture, movies, TV, and other sources that don't reflect God's plan.

God has asked men to be good husbands to their wives, to be good fathers to their children, to provide for and protect their families, and to lead their families spiritually in God's Word.

As your dad, do you think I reflect the description of a godly man? *(If Dad isn't leading the devotion, change how you ask the question. Encourage responses.)*

Let's discuss what I can do better to be the man God wants me to be.

(If you have sons in your family, ask this question: What can you do better to become who God wants you to be as a man?)

MANHOOD

SCRIPTURE READING: PROVERBS 27:17

Today we'll look at some functions and roles God has set for men in His creation. God's design for men and women is a bit like sports, where different players play in different positions for the good of the team. Let's see what God's Word has to say about manhood.

Be alert, stand firm in the faith, act like a man, be strong.
I CORINTHIANS 16:13

The husband is the head of the wife as Christ is the head of the church. He is the Savior of the body. EPHESIANS 5:23

Husbands, love your wives, just as Christ loved the church and gave Himself for her. EPHESIANS 5:25

An overseer, then, must be above reproach, the husband of one wife, temperate, prudent, respectable, hospitable, able to teach, not addicted to wine or pugnacious, but gentle, peaceable, free from the love of money. He must be one who manages his own household well, keeping his children under control with all dignity (but if a man does not know how to manage his own household, how will he take care of the church of God?). I TIMOTHY 3:2–5, NASB

Husbands . . . , live with your wives in an understanding way, as with someone weaker, since she is a woman; and show her honor as a fellow heir of the grace of life, so that your prayers will not be hindered. I PETER 3:7, NASB

According to these verses, what does God want a kingdom man to do? Now, of course, women should also be respectable and hospitable, but our focus this week is on the roles of men in God's kingdom.

Let's pray together and ask God to give us wisdom and understanding as we learn more about His design for men and women, boys and girls.

MANHOOD

Scripture Reading: Job 15:14

What do you know about the role of the quarterback on a football team? *(Allow time for discussion.)* A quarterback is the team leader, who makes sure the offense is lined up correctly and that team members know and understand the plays. He also takes responsibility for delivering the football to the right players in order to score touchdowns.

When a team loses a game, the quarterback usually takes the blame because of his position as leader. He's ultimately responsible for how the team performs. It goes with the job.

Like a quarterback, men have an important position of responsibility in marriage. Manhood means the husband is responsible even if he isn't to blame for problems in the marriage or family. Each family member depends on him to make the right calls so the whole family can go in the right direction. Manhood means being the quarterback of the family simply because it's the man's position.

Let's think of some examples where a husband needs to take responsibility in a marriage. *(Come prepared to share at least one example of your own.)*

Should both a husband and a wife give their ideas and opinions before decisions are made? *(Allow time for discussion.)* The answer is yes. What would happen if a husband and a wife didn't have the opportunity to share their opinions about a decision?

If a decision has to be made, but the husband and wife disagree, who should make the ultimate decision? *(Explain that it's similar to a football team where the quarterback ultimately calls the plays.)*

If that decision goes wrong, who will be held responsible? Remember, responsibility carries a lot of power and influence, but it also means owning up when things go wrong.

MANHOOD

Scripture Reading: 1 Corinthians 16:13–14

Learning how to be a kingdom man is a big responsibility. Let's look at four things a godly man should know and do:*

1. *Being a gentleman is still worth the effort.* A gentleman holds the door for a lady and stands up when she leaves the room or joins the table. He also walks on the "splash" side of the sidewalk. *(If you have sons, add the following activity: Let's practice some of these behaviors right now. The gentlemen in the room will stand up when the ladies leave or sit down at the table. We'll run through this a few times so you can get used to it.)*

2. *Be respectful.* All of the "gentlemanly" actions just listed must be offered subtly and, if necessary, set aside graciously when refused.

3. *Take responsibility.* In a word (well, two), "step up." True manhood means that a gentleman takes responsibility for his actions, choices, values, and beliefs. It also means being willing to admit, with grace, when he's wrong.

4. *Listen respectfully, disagree politely, and never exclude ladies from the conversation.* True manhood is inclusive. It may be strong, but it's unfailingly polite. *(If you have sons, practice listening and speaking politely. Introduce the activity as follows: Start a conversation right now. It can be about anything—new activities at school, last Sunday's church sermon, a game, or a great movie or TV show you just saw. The gentlemen in the room should give equal or more time to the ladies when they speak. A godly gentleman always listens with respect and kindness.)*

---

* Summarized from Jeffrey Marx, *Season of Life* (New York: Simon and Schuster, 2003).

WOMANHOOD

SCRIPTURE READING: PROVERBS 14:1

God has laid out certain roles for women in His Word. But the world is as open to a woman (or girl), as it is to any man (or boy).

As a girl grows into a woman, she can experience the fullness of womanhood by learning to feel comfortable speaking her mind. Sometimes boys get more attention because they speak louder or move around more in class. Some girls may do the same, while others can make themselves heard in their own individual ways.

Boys and girls also act differently sometimes. But a girl's thoughts carry a lot of value. The way girls see the world and the insights God gives them contribute to others. People need to hear what they have to say. They shouldn't have to keep their mouths closed simply because a boy might be talking louder.

Science has proved that men and women not only have different bodies, but their brains also function differently. Rather than trying to be something or someone they're not, women need to look for how they can make the most of their potential by being exactly who they are.

Let's give the ladies in our family some practice speaking their minds. *(If you have only one female in the family, modify your words accordingly.)* Once you've decided who's going first, choose a subject you want to talk about. *(Brainstorm a list of ideas for discussion.)*

You'll get a minute or two to share your thoughts and ideas while the rest of us listen. When you're done talking, we'll ask questions about what you said. Since we want this to be a respectful discussion, we won't allow any questions intended for argument or disagreement.

(Have fun with this activity. If the speaker is interrupted, go back to the start of the conversation and try again.)

WOMANHOOD

SCRIPTURE READING: PROVERBS 31:10–31

This week we're learning about womanhood. A woman expresses true womanhood by first listening to God, so she can live her life in obedience to Him.

To put it another way, for a woman to truly be a kingdom woman, she should be obedient to God, just as children are to be obedient to their parents. God has asked women to respect their husbands, love and care for their children, manage the home, and teach their daughters and other young women to behave in the same way.

Before we talked about true womanhood, what did you think a real woman should be? Were any of your ideas based on our pop culture, music, or media? What about advertisements and commercials? *(Contrast common cultural definitions of womanhood with the biblical definition of what a godly woman should be.)*

Do you think Mom meets the description of a godly woman? Let's discuss what she can do better to be the woman God wants her to be. *(If you have daughters, ask the following question: What can you do to grow into the woman God wants you to be?)*

Let's pray together and ask God to help us learn and grow this week as we spend time on the subject of biblical womanhood.

WOMANHOOD

SCRIPTURE READING: PROVERBS 19:14

God tells us a lot in His Word about being a godly woman. Let's read what He has to say.

Every wise woman builds her house, but a foolish one tears it down with her own hands. PROVERBS 14:1

Who can find a capable wife? She is far more precious than jewels. The heart of her husband trusts in her, and he will not lack anything good. PROVERBS 31:10–11

Wives, submit to your own husbands as to the Lord, for the husband is the head of the wife as Christ is the head of the church. He is the Savior of the body. Now as the church submits to Christ, so wives are to submit to their husbands in everything. EPHESIANS 5:22–24

Older women are to be reverent in behavior, not slanderers, not addicted to much wine. They are to teach what is good, so they may encourage the young women to love their husbands and to love their children, to be self-controlled, pure, homemakers, kind, and submissive to their husbands, so that God's message will not be slandered. TITUS 2:3–5

There are many more Bible passages about womanhood, but these give us a good peek into God's heart regarding the way He desires women to live.

What do we learn from these verses about what happens if and when a woman doesn't live according to God's Word? *(The verse in Titus says that her life will slander God's message.)*

Womanhood is about so much more than living out personal goals and dreams. God wants women to reflect His image and message in all they do and say. Women have a high calling as daughters of the King, reflecting Him everywhere they go.

WOMANHOOD

SCRIPTURE READING: TITUS 2:3–5

If you've ever gone to a florist shop, you've probably noticed a huge price difference between carnations and roses. You can buy a dozen carnations for just a few dollars, but a few dollars will only buy one rose.

Why do roses cost so much more than carnations? Because the sweet fragrance of roses lasts much longer and adds to their value. Carnations are pretty and plentiful, but their fragrance just doesn't last very long.

Some women in our world today have settled for being carnations. They've found value in the way they look and dress, in the style of their hair, and in other external things that don't reflect the truth about womanhood.

Women who focus only on their looks devalue their own worth. They've chosen a "carnation life" instead of expressing the long-lasting fragrance of a rose. Women who are concerned only about appearance are plentiful in our world, but they lack the qualities of those who care most about reflecting God's love and the beauty they have on the inside.

True womanhood isn't about how a woman looks; it's about how she lives.

What is one way a woman can let her inner beauty shine through?

Let's talk about women who are role models that demonstrate godly hearts and lives. Why do these women stand out to you?

God calls kingdom women to live out the roles He created for them.

WOMANHOOD

SCRIPTURE READING: 1 PETER 3:1

It isn't wrong for women to want to look their best. But God calls them to be so much more than what the world sees on the outside. Let's read what God's Word has to say about beauty.

Your beauty should not consist of outward things like elaborate hairstyles and the wearing of gold ornaments or fine clothes. Instead, it should consist of what is inside the heart with the imperishable quality of a gentle and quiet spirit, which is very valuable in God's eyes. For in the past, the holy women who put their hope in God also beautified themselves in this way, submitting to their own husbands, just as Sarah obeyed Abraham, calling him lord. You have become her children when you do what is good and are not frightened by anything alarming. 1 PETER 3:3–6

That's saying an awful lot in one passage, isn't it? God wants women to focus on their hearts and on having gentle and quiet spirits. He tells us very clearly that a gentle and quiet spirit in a woman is "very valuable in [His] eyes."

What are some ways a woman can have a gentle and quiet spirit? What does that look like?

(If you have daughters, ask the following question: How can you respond with a gentle and quiet spirit to someone who upsets you?)

Do you know a woman who has a gentle and quiet spirit? Describe that person and what you like best about her.

The ultimate definition of a woman is found in her heart and spirit. In God's eyes, a woman who fears Him—to fear God means to take Him seriously and put Him first in our lives—is to be praised (Proverbs 31:30).

SIN

SCRIPTURE READING: JAMES 4:17

Salvation is *good* news, but it comes to us against a backdrop of *bad* news. The bad news is that we're all sinners. Not one person in the world today is without sin.

In the original Greek, the New Testament word for "sin" meant "to miss the mark," like an archer who fails to hit a target. What is the target we miss when we sin? Romans 3:23 says, "All have sinned and *fall short of the glory of God*" (emphasis added). Sin is falling short of God's glory: His standard.

Sin isn't measured by big or little failures to miss the target. Either we fall short of God's glory or we don't. Since the entire sin question rests on this point, let's make sure we understand our target: God's standard of righteousness.

Did you know that "it is a sin for the person who knows to do what is good and doesn't do it" (James 4:17)? If you or I know to do something good for someone or for God but don't do it, it's a sin. Unfortunately, it's very easy to sin. That's why we should be grateful to Jesus Christ, who died to give us salvation.

Let's play a game. First, we'll position a pillow (or another soft object) on one side of the room. That's the target. Next we'll roll up a paper towel or sock to throw at the pillow. Let's take turns trying to hit the pillow. Then try to miss it. Is there any difference between missing the target by a lot and missing it by just a little?

Sin is the same way. When we fail to live according to God's standard of right and wrong, based on His rule of love, we have missed His mark, whether we miss it by a little or by a lot.

SIN

SCRIPTURE READING: 1 JOHN 1:8–10

This week we're learning about sin. Sin is when we disobey God's Word in the things we do, say, and think. This includes lying, stealing, fighting, wanting what someone else has, and many other attitudes and behaviors that are the opposite of what God wants for us.

We want to learn about sin not just because sinning is wrong but because it gets in the way of a good relationship with God. Isn't it hard to be close to someone who's always hurting our feelings? Some of the things we do hurt God's feelings. Let's list some examples right now.

If we want to grow in our relationship with God, we need to work on being more like Him instead of doing things that hurt Him. What are some ways we can work on becoming more like Jesus instead of doing those things? *(Brainstorm a list of ideas.)*

Accepting Jesus Christ is the only way to deal with the problem of sin and be brought back into relationship with God. Jesus Christ credited His perfect righteousness to those who believe in Him so that we can live in perfect harmony with God in heaven. But we still have a responsibility on a day-to-day basis to remove sin from our lives so that our relationship with God can grow stronger right here on Earth.

One thing we can do is pray. Let's talk to God right now about our desire to be more like Him and live the way He guides us to live in His Word.

SIN

SCRIPTURE READING: ROMANS 6:23

L et's read and discuss what God has to say about the subject of sin.

The wages of sin is death, but the gift of God is eternal life in Christ Jesus our Lord. ROMANS 6:23

Sin brings about death in ways you might not realize. It could be the death of a dream. Or the death of a relationship that used to be close and good. It could be the death of this afternoon's plans because you're now grounded in your room. But it also means eternal death, which is why Jesus died on the cross, so our sins can be forgiven and we can have eternal life.

If we say, "We have no sin," we are deceiving ourselves, and the truth is not in us. 1 JOHN 1:8

Does everyone sin? Give some examples of sins.

All have sinned and fall short of the glory of God. ROMANS 3:23

The Bible says that Jesus never sinned. *(Some Scriptures you can read aloud are 2 Corinthians 5:21, Hebrews 4:15, and 1 John 3:5.)* Is there anyone besides Jesus who has never sinned?

Submit . . . to God. Resist the devil and he will flee from you. JAMES 4:7, NASB

What does God tell us to do to keep ourselves from sinning?

Walk by the Spirit, and you will not carry out the desire of the flesh. GALATIANS 5:16, NASB

What does it mean to "walk by the Spirit"?

[God] made the One who did not know sin to be sin for us, so that we might become the righteousness of God in Him. 2 CORINTHIANS 5:21

How did Jesus, who never sinned, become sin for us? How does that make you feel?

SIN

SCRIPTURE READING: ROMANS 3:23

Every sport has rules to follow in order to win. Usually, if you don't follow the rules, you get a penalty that stops you or your team from moving forward or scoring points.

In football, when a player is penalized, the whole team loses yardage. If you jump offside in football, the team has to back up five yards. If you commit a holding penalty, the team loses ten yards. If it's a personal-foul penalty, the team has to back up fifteen yards. Every penalty has a different consequence, but each penalty sends the team backward. To move forward, team members have to follow the playbook without breaking the rules.

Sin is simply breaking the rules of the playbook, called the Bible, while playing the game of life. Whenever you sin against God, you not only stop yourself from moving forward to where He wants you to be, but you actually go backward, away from accomplishing His purposes for your life. While you can control the sin, you cannot control the consequences of sin. Each sin brings about its own consequences, and those consequences are all different and specific.

Let's illustrate this concept with a game. Everyone stand in line except for one person, who will be the leader. The leader will give directions to everyone, such as stand on one foot, jump up and down, turn in circles, recite the alphabet, and so on. We'll take turns being the person who does *not* follow the leader's directions. That person has to jog in place for the rest of the game.

(When you're finished playing the game, explain how the consequences of sin often stay with us, making it harder for us to become who God intended us to be.)

SIN

SCRIPTURE READING: ROMANS 5:19

Two men were exploring an island when suddenly a volcano erupted. In moments the men found themselves surrounded by molten lava. A clearing and a path to safety were several feet away. To get there, however, they would have to jump across the river of melted rock.

The first man was an active senior citizen, but he was hardly an outstanding physical specimen. He ran as fast as he could and took an admirable leap, but he traveled only a few feet. He met a swift death in the superheated lava.

The other explorer was a much younger, more physically fit man in excellent shape. In fact, the college record he had set in the broad jump had remained unbroken to that day. He put all his energy into his run, jumped with flawless form, and shattered his own college record. Unfortunately he landed far short of the clearing. Though the younger man clearly outperformed his companion, both wound up dead. Survival was too far out of reach, so individual ability became a nonissue.

Degrees of goodness may be important when hiring an employee or choosing neighbors or getting awards in school. But when the issue is sin, the only standard that matters is God's perfect holiness.

The question isn't how you measure up against the kid down the street or even other family members but how you measure up to God's perfect standard of righteousness. It's a standard that even the best-behaved person in the world can't reach.

Why don't we all spend some time in prayer right now, thanking Jesus for providing a perfect sacrifice for our sins.

FORGIVENESS

SCRIPTURE READING: MARK 11:25

Forgiveness is important because it reflects the heart of God, who sacrificed His Son so our sins could be forgiven. When we don't forgive others, we aren't modeling God's heart, and the unforgiveness inside us grows into something called bitterness. Bitterness can make us grumpy, angry, or hateful and affect what we say to the people around us.

When someone has sinned against you, it causes a wound in your soul. If that wound is left untreated, it may not heal, and it will continue to hurt and be sensitive to the slightest touch.

Unforgiveness has the same effect (see Matthew 18:34-35). When the wounds in our souls are left untreated, they cause pain in other areas of our lives. Then even the slightest brush from someone else can cause us to react in ways we normally wouldn't. We overreact. We may lash out, accuse, blame, cry, or say and do things we regret later.

Let's act out what it often looks like when unforgiveness is allowed to fester. One person will pretend that you've been called bad names or been put down, and you haven't forgiven the offender. Another family member will come up and tell that person how to do better on a report or an art project. Keep in mind, the person giving advice isn't being mean but is just trying to be helpful. But the person receiving the advice was hurt in the past by another person's unkind words, so he or she will overreact.

(After family members act out the scenario a few times, and everyone understands what's going on, it will be easier to see the role of forgiveness in their daily lives.)

Forgiveness is really important, because when we don't forgive, our pain spills out onto others who never did anything to us and don't deserve our hurtful words or actions.

To overcome unforgiveness, treat your wounds and let them heal.

FORGIVENESS

SCRIPTURE READING: EPHESIANS 4:32

This week we're learning about forgiveness. It's important to forgive people because God has forgiven us. We want to show people the love God has shown us, even if we sometimes feel they don't deserve it. If we want God to forgive us, we must be willing to forgive others.

Do you remember a time when a friend or family member hurt you? What happened? *(Encourage each family member to share a story. Be prepared to share one of your own.)* Did you feel that what that person did or said was unforgivable? Do you still feel that way? Does that experience still cause you pain? Let's pray right now about forgiving that person so you can begin the process of forgiveness. *(Spend time in prayer together.)*

Remember, if Christ can forgive us for what we've done to Him, we should be able to forgive others for what they do to us. What most people don't understand is that unforgiveness holds them hostage to the hurt they've experienced.

FORGIVENESS

SCRIPTURE READING: MATTHEW 6:15

L et's see what God's Word tells us about forgiveness.

Hatred stirs up conflicts, but love covers all offenses.   PROVERBS 10:12

If you forgive people their wrongdoing, your heavenly Father will forgive you as well. But if you don't forgive people, your Father will not forgive your wrongdoing.   MATTHEW 6:14–15

Peter came to [Jesus] and said, "Lord, how many times could my brother sin against me and I forgive him? As many as seven times?"
    "I tell you, not as many as seven," Jesus said to him, "but 70 times seven."   MATTHEW 18:21–22

Be kind and compassionate to one another, forgiving one another, just as God also forgave you in Christ.   EPHESIANS 4:32

[Accept] one another and [forgive] one another if anyone has a complaint against another. Just as the Lord has forgiven you, so you must also forgive.   COLOSSIANS 3:13

God is very concerned with this area of our lives, isn't He? This is because He sacrificed His very own Son on the cross, giving His all to forgive us! So He isn't happy when we refuse to forgive someone who has wronged us.

Always remember to forgive. Never hold a grudge. No one is perfect. Just as we all need to be forgiven, so we should always forgive.

FORGIVENESS

SCRIPTURE READING: 1 JOHN 1:9

Kelly was sitting in her kindergarten class. She was nervous because it was her turn to go to the whiteboard and answer math questions in front of the class.

She was afraid of making a mistake, but it was time for her to pick up the red marker and write "2 + 3 =" on the board. Then the teacher asked Kelly to write the correct answer for everyone to see. The little girl counted on her fingers and then wrote 6.

When the teacher told Kelly that was the wrong answer, Kelly began to cry.

"Try again," said the teacher.

"How can I try again when the mistake is already on the board?" Kelly asked.

The teacher explained that a whiteboard is very forgiving; it makes it easy to erase mistakes. She then easily wiped away Kelly's wrong answer.

Like a whiteboard, the work of Jesus Christ has made it easy to erase every sin or mistake we've ever made, leaving our lives squeaky clean. All we have to do is believe in Him and ask Him to forgive our sins, and we'll have a fresh start.

To help us remember this, let's try a little experiment. Someone write down the word *mistake* on a piece of paper. Now someone else erase it. Make sure you erase it really well. When you're finished, tell everyone what you see.

Let's be glad that Jesus is able to wipe away our sins before God so that when He looks at us, He sees the righteousness of His Son instead of our mistakes and sin. We just need to ask Him for forgiveness.

FORGIVENESS

SCRIPTURE READING: MATTHEW 18:21–22

Forgiving others isn't always easy to do, especially when we feel hurt. Did you know you can *choose* to forgive even when you don't feel like it? Forgiveness is a choice you make not to hold a grudge against the person who wronged you. You can choose to let it go and move on.

When you forgive someone, you aren't saying that what that person did was fine. You aren't letting that person off the hook. Instead, you're letting God handle things. Forgiveness has to come from a heart of love because of what God has done for you. Otherwise you probably won't be able to do it, since the offense hurt so much.

Today's Fun Friday activity is going to emphasize what it means to forgive. Get a piece of paper and write about a time when someone hurt you. Describe what that person did and how it made you feel. After we've finished, everyone will tear up our papers. Rip them to shreds! Then we'll toss them in a trash can or even go outside, dig a hole, and bury them.

That's the first step in letting go of the wrongs done to you. The second step is to pray and ask God to put a special forgiving love in your heart for the person who hurt you. Ask for His help, because forgiveness is such a hard thing to do. We all need God's help when it comes to forgiving someone who has hurt us.

You might feel the pain the person caused for a while, but give it time. With God's help and your decision to forgive, your wounds will begin to heal!

WITNESSING

SCRIPTURE READING: 1 PETER 3:15

Telling others about Jesus is called *witnessing*. You can witness to others in any number of ways. It doesn't always mean sitting down with them, pulling out a Bible, and walking them through the Scriptures. Did you know you can be a witness for Jesus by the way you live?

When you obey God's Word in your life, you're a witness. When a friend at school sees you treat someone with kindness or respect, you're being a witness of Christ's love inside you.

Let's act out a situation where one family member witnesses to another without using words. Take a moment to decide what you'll do and how you'll do it. When we're finished with the role playing, we'll talk about whether the message of God's love got communicated.

Jesus not only wants you to be a witness of His love and God's goodness to those around you; He also wants you to tell others about His saving love when you can. That might be as simple as sharing a Bible verse with a friend. Do you have John 3:16 memorized? If you don't, try to memorize it this week. Let's say it together: "For God so loved the world, that He gave His only begotten Son, that whoever believes in Him shall not perish, but have eternal life" (NASB).

That one verse sums up what it takes to be saved: believing in the Lord Jesus Christ for the forgiveness of sins. Jesus died on the cross as a sacrifice for our sins, so when you tell someone about that, you're witnessing about Jesus and His free gift of salvation.

WITNESSING

SCRIPTURE READING: MARK 16:15–16

This week we're learning about witnessing. Witnessing means sharing our belief in Jesus Christ with other people. When we witness, we get to pass along good news to others: Jesus Christ died on the cross for our sins and then rose from the dead so that we might be saved.

Good news is something we like to share with other people. Do you have any friends you think would want to hear good news? Who needs to hear the good news of Jesus Christ?

Let's learn to tell about the best news in the world. For today's family activity, let's list up to ten individuals we know who may not know Jesus Christ or may not have heard the good news about His love for us. What are some creative ways we can introduce these people to Jesus Christ?

As we talk and share ideas, we'll write down a plan of action for each family member to carry out in the near future.

Let's close our time together by praying about these plans and asking God to help us fulfill them. We want to be people who share good news with others!

WITNESSING

SCRIPTURE READING: COLOSSIANS 4:6

L et's dive in and read God's Word to better understand His heart for us on the subject of witnessing.

Then Jesus came near and said to [His disciples], "All authority has been given to Me in heaven and on earth. Go, therefore, and make disciples of all nations, baptizing them in the name of the Father and of the Son and of the Holy Spirit, teaching them to observe everything I have commanded you. And remember, I am with you always, to the end of the age." MATTHEW 28:18–20

[Jesus] said to [His disciples], "Go into all the world and preach the gospel to the whole creation. Whoever believes and is baptized will be saved, but whoever does not believe will be condemned." MARK 16:15–16

I am not ashamed of the gospel, because it is God's power for salvation to everyone who believes, first to the Jew, and also to the Greek. ROMANS 1:16

It sure does sound like God is serious when it comes to wanting us to tell others about Him, doesn't it?

What is one way you could share Jesus with the people around you? How do you feel when you think about doing that? Does it make you excited, nervous, or afraid? *(Encourage discussion.)*

I hope we're all thrilled and excited about having an opportunity to tell others about our Lord and savior Jesus Christ! Let's pray together and ask God to give us the desire and courage to share Jesus with others.

WITNESSING

SCRIPTURE READING: ROMANS 1:16

Golden-winged warblers are birds that can sense a storm coming up to two days before it arrives. When they know a storm is coming, they begin communicating with one another and even alert other birds. After a while they all leave the area and fly together to a place of safety.

Some species of birds don't listen to the signals of the golden-winged warblers, probably because they don't understand the message. However, all of the golden-winged warblers, and any other birds that do understand, heed the warning and fly out of danger.

As a Christian, you may sense that without Jesus Christ, people have a big problem. What is one thing that can happen to people who don't know Jesus? *(Encourage everyone to answer.)* Lots of things can happen, but one of the most important involves where people will spend eternity. It won't be in heaven if they don't know and trust in Jesus. I'd call that a really big storm, wouldn't you?

Knowing this can motivate us to tell people about Jesus. Like the golden-winged warbler, we can warn them of the upcoming storm of spending eternity without God.

Have you ever told someone about salvation in Jesus Christ? What happened? How did you feel about it?

Let's practice telling others about salvation in Jesus. Pretend that another family member is a new kid you met in school that you've just run into. How would you share the gospel with that person?

Let's take turns, with one of us sharing the good news and another person hearing it.

Let's pray together, asking God for the opportunity to tell more people about salvation in Jesus.

WITNESSING

SCRIPTURE READING: MATTHEW 5:16

Witnessing doesn't have to be difficult. You don't have to say everything perfectly. The basics include the fact that we're all sinners, yet we must meet God's standard in order to enter into heaven after we die, and that standard is perfection. Since none of us are perfect, He sent His sinless Son, Jesus Christ, to pay the price for our sins. Jesus did this on the cross when He died and rose again. To be saved from our sins, we need to trust in Jesus Christ's sacrifice by believing in Him and confessing our sins and our need for a savior.

Today's Fun Friday activity will show us that witnessing can be fun. First, we'll get a big bowl from the kitchen and put water into it. *(Or go outside if there's a little wading pool—or even a big pool.)* We're going to put something in the water. As the parents, we get to choose what that will be—maybe we'll put rocks or eggs in the bowl.

Each of us will take turns sharing one part of the gospel message with another family member. As you share something about Jesus, you'll retrieve whatever is in the water. Let's practice this until nothing is left in the water.

It's okay to share the same thing more than once. This activity will help plant these important gospel truths deep in your heart so they'll be easier for you to remember.

Have fun sharing Jesus with other family members! Then when God gives you an opportunity to tell someone else about Him, you'll be prepared to do it. Remember this fun activity when you do. It will help you not be nervous!

Let's pray, thanking God for the opportunity to tell others about the joy of knowing Jesus Christ and His salvation!

IDOLATRY

SCRIPTURE READING: EXODUS 20:3–6

*I*dolatry is a really big word, and it can be a difficult concept to understand. But it's based on a very simple truth: An idol is any person, thought, or thing we hold in our hearts that's more important to us than God.

Can you name some idols? *(Encourage responses.)*

Is TV an idol? If you had a choice to watch TV or read your Bible, which would you choose? Does that mean the activity you chose is more important to you than the other one?

Lots of people think an idol is a woodcarving, a statue, a tree that is worshipped, or even a rabbit's foot hanging from a car's rearview mirror. But an idol doesn't have to be an object. It can be a person you value more than God.

How can you know when you're making a person, thought, or thing an idol? *(Allow time for discussion.)* Here are just a few ways you can know:

- When you let a person, thought, or thing take you away from what God would have you do and how He would have you live.
- When you make what that person says, or whether or not that person likes you, more important than pleasing God.
- When you make that thing—such as a video game or a TV show—more important than God.
- When you spend so much time with that person or thing that you give up time with God.
- When you focus your heart's joy and happiness on your "idol" instead of on what God wants for your life.

Let's talk about ways to get rid of idols and put God back where He belongs in our lives.

IDOLATRY

SCRIPTURE READING: JONAH 2:8

This week we're learning about idolatry. When we place anything or anyone above God in our lives, we're practicing idolatry. When we no longer depend on God to provide for us, we're depending on other things to meet our needs instead of God. God is no longer the primary object of our faith and trust.

God wants to be the one we call on when we're in need, and He wants us to let Him be first in our lives. We don't want to let money, fame, power, or anything else take the place of God in our lives, because all of those other things will fail us.

God made this clear in the first of the Ten Commandments: "Do not have other gods besides Me" (Exodus 20:3).

For today's family discussion, let's answer a few questions.

What are some things, places, or people that seem to have taken God's place in our culture?

What do you need God to help you with? Do you really believe He can help, or do you think someone or something else could help you better? Why?

No one else can help us better than God can. So let's trust Him and keep Him first in our lives.

Why don't we pray together right now, thanking God for His love and care and asking for His help to recognize and get rid of the idols in our lives?

IDOLATRY

SCRIPTURE READING: 1 JOHN 5:21

The Bible has a lot to say about idolatry. When it comes to being first in our lives, God doesn't mess around. That's exactly where He wants to be and deserves to be. After all, He put us first when He gave His one and only Son as a sacrifice to die on the cross for our sins. And He takes care of us each and every day. Let's read what God says about idolatry.

Do not have other gods besides Me. Do not make an idol for yourself, whether in the shape of anything in the heavens above or on the earth below or in the waters under the earth. You must not bow down to them or worship them; for I, the LORD your God, am a jealous God, punishing the children for the fathers' sin, to the third and fourth generations of those who hate Me, but showing faithful love to a thousand generations of those who love Me and keep My commands. EXODUS 20:3–6

My dear friends, flee from idolatry. 1 CORINTHIANS 10:14

In the past, when you didn't know God, you were enslaved to things that by nature are not gods. GALATIANS 4:8

Little children, guard yourselves from idols. 1 JOHN 5:21

What do these verses tell us about idols? (God is jealous for our worship and wants us to worship Him alone. God wants us to run away from them. Idols make us slaves.)

What are some of the idols people have today?

Is there a way to enjoy something or someone without making that thing or person an idol? What would that look like in our lives, thoughts, and choices?

Would you be willing to give up something you truly value if God asked you to? Why or why not?

IDOLATRY

SCRIPTURE READING: PSALM 135:15–18

Jimmy loves playing and watching basketball. His favorite player of all is LeBron James. Eighteen-year-old Jimmy wants to be just like LeBron on and off the court. He wants to wear the same kinds of shoes, grow to a height of six feet eight inches, and play basketball just like LeBron. You could say that Jimmy wants to be the spitting image of his idol.

There are, however, a few problems for Jimmy when it comes to being just like LeBron James. Jimmy isn't gifted at playing basketball. He can't shoot, dribble, play defense, or dunk the ball like his idol. Jimmy is also only five feet five inches tall, and he's about finished growing. It seems pretty clear that Jimmy isn't going to be anything like LeBron James. He's trying to make himself over in the image of someone he can never be like. For Jimmy, idolizing LeBron James is simply keeping him from becoming the young man God created him to be.

Many Christians today are just like Jimmy. They spend their time trying to imitate people they can never, and should never, be like. As Christians, we're to imitate God's Son, Jesus Christ.

Let's name some popular celebrities or athletes that people today try to resemble.

Is there anyone you model yourself after or hope to be like one day?

What is the difference between looking up to someone as a mentor and looking at that person as an idol?

What are some ways we can imitate Jesus? Let's pray together and ask Him to make us more like Him each day.

IDOLATRY

SCRIPTURE READING: PSALM 16:4

We've been talking about what idols look like and how they can become more important in our lives than God. God is a jealous God, and He doesn't want anything to be more important to us than He is.

For today's Fun Friday activity, we're going to start by gathering some paper, crayons, scissors, and other supplies to make a craft. We might want to go outside and collect leaves or sticks as well.

When we've gathered our supplies, we're going to make what would have been considered idols in times past. You might make an idol that looks like a statue or some other figure. Or you can draw idols you've seen in books. Remember, you're making an idol from Bible times, so it probably won't look like the idols we have today.

After we're finished, we'll talk about, draw, or create things that might be idols in our lives today. That could be a girl or a boy you have a crush on. Or it could be a video game. Yes, it could even be a sport you play. What do we sometimes put ahead of God in our hearts and lives?

Now compare the two idols you made. They probably look very different. It's easy to say and think you don't have an idol in your life when you look at the first idol. But when you look at the second, it's more difficult, isn't it? Keep this in mind in the days ahead.

Always keep God first in your heart and then you'll be able to enjoy everything else. That's the right order.

TRUTH

SCRIPTURE READING: JOHN 14:6

Jesus is all about truth. He said in John 8:32, "You will know the truth, and the truth will set you free."

Take a moment to find a scarf, shoestrings, a rope, or anything else you can use to tie another family member's hands together. Once you've tied up the other person, allow him or her to struggle to get free. Once several of us have done this, we'll discuss how it feels to be bound and how wonderful freedom is.

What is truth? *Truth* is defined as "God's view of a matter." It's what God says. The presence of God's truth brings understanding and victory, but the absence of it brings confusion and defeat. Truth is powerful, isn't it?

Truth is made up of information and facts, but it also includes God's original intent or purpose. It's God's absolute standard by which we can measure everything else.

Here's a story that will help explain why truth is more than just facts. A man went fishing and brought home twenty catfish. He told his wife, "Honey, I caught twenty catfish today." That was a fact. He had the twenty catfish he'd caught.

His wife, however, knew he wasn't a very good fisherman, so she asked him, "How did you catch twenty catfish?"

He answered, "Well, I went to the fish market and asked the guy to toss me twenty catfish. And I caught them all!"

This man gave his wife the facts, but he didn't give her the truth. He hid the facts in his "truth."

Truth always includes more than the facts. It includes the meaning—or purpose—behind the facts. So let's be careful to tell the truth from our hearts and not just with our words.

TRUTH

SCRIPTURE READING: JOHN 8:32

This week we're talking about truth. Truth is like math: Every math equation has an answer, and that answer can't ever be changed.

For example, one plus one equals two. That math equation will always have the same answer because the answer is true. Truth doesn't change, no matter what you feel or what other people say. God's Word shows us what is true, and as long as we live by the truth, we'll understand the correct equations and answers in life.

Living your life by doing what God says will always keep things true, even if it doesn't feel like it sometimes. Let's answer a few true-and-false questions. Write down your answers quietly on a sheet of paper.

1. Children should obey their parents. True or false?
2. Children should learn to share with others. True or false?
3. Children should be honest and always tell the truth. True or false?

The answers to all three questions are true!

The Bible says to obey your parents, share with others, and be honest. These things are true. Remember, truth isn't something you get to decide on your own; it's something that already exists outside of your personal preferences.

As Christians we believe that the Bible is the Word of God, and since God is perfect, His Word is perfectly true. Our job as Christians isn't to follow our hearts. Our job is to make our hearts follow the truth.

Let's pray together and ask God to help us learn His truth and follow it no matter what.

TRUTH

SCRIPTURE READING: JOHN 16:13

How can you figure out what's true? How do you know whether something is true? Do your feelings tell you what is true? Feelings change—sometimes you're up, sometimes you're down; sometimes you're happy, sometimes you're sad.

What if I told you I was going to give you a million dollars? Your feelings might fly high as you think, *I'll be rich! I'll be able to buy anything I want!* But what if I told you that the million dollars was just play money? You'd probably scream or get pretty upset with me!

We need to understand our feelings because they're real, but they should never be our main guide for figuring out the truth. It's all too easy to let this world and the people in it lead us to believe truths other than the truth of God's Word. But only God is the creator of truth. Knowing Him and His Word is the only way to live in truth.

Let's read what God says in His Word about truth.

The LORD is near all who call out to Him, all who call out to Him with integrity. PSALM 145:18

Jesus told [Thomas], "I am the way, the truth, and the life. No one comes to the Father except through Me." JOHN 14:6

When the Spirit of truth comes, He will guide you into all the truth. JOHN 16:13

Sanctify them by the truth; Your word is truth. JOHN 17:17

Let's pray together and thank God for teaching us His truth.

TRUTH

SCRIPTURE READING: JOHN 17:17

A Sunday school teacher came to class one Sunday with a jar full of M&M's. She stated that just as there was an exact number of M&M's in the jar, truth is an exact standard. She asked the students to write down how many M&M's they thought were in the jar and told them she was the only one who knew the exact number because she counted them before bringing them to class.

One by one the students walked to the front of the room to turn in their guesses. One student, Nikki, was still staring at the jar, trying to figure out the exact number. Finally, before writing her guess on the paper, she raised her hand and asked the teacher. "Miss Turner, how many M&M's are in the jar?"

Miss Turner answered, "There are exactly 589 M&M's in the jar."

Nikki wrote down the answer, and she was the only one who got it right. Everyone else got it wrong. She didn't know the answer, but she got it right simply because she asked the teacher.

Jesus Christ is the only teacher who knows the truth and is the truth. Sometimes we make things more difficult than they really are. God tells us that if we lack wisdom, all we need to do is ask, and He'll give it to us. Wisdom is found in truth.

Let's play a game to help us remember today's lesson. First we'll find a jar and fill it with candy, marbles, or rocks from outside. Next we'll take turns guessing how many items are in each person's jar. The one whose guess is closest to the correct answer will be declared the official winner!

TRUTH

SCRIPTURE READING: PSALM 119:16

Truth doesn't change with the latest fashion or fad. One plus one will always equal two. Even when we feel like we want it to equal three, one plus one still equals two. Even if we hope, believe, and claim that one plus one should equal three, one plus one will never equal three because we can't change the laws of mathematics!

Truth is a powerful reality that God has predetermined—or chosen. Our thoughts and actions need to line up with His truth. This is what it means to live under God's kingdom agenda. It means bringing our thoughts and actions in line with His truth and placing ourselves under His rule.

We need to make sure that what's on the inside *and* the outside reflects God's truth. That includes our thoughts, attitudes, actions, decisions, conversations, and choices.

God knows when we're faking it. After all, He already knows everything about us. He knows when we're hiding something from Him. We can't shock God. We can't surprise Him. He already knows it all.

For today's Fun Friday activity, let's go around the room and say one truthful thing about someone else in our family. Now be sure it's a *positive* truthful thing! Then we'll play a game called Truth or Trick. Each of us gets to say two things about ourselves, and the rest of us have to guess which statement is true and which is the trick.

For example, the truth might be that I love to snow ski. My trick might be I fought a bear.

You can make it silly if you want to! It's a good way to practice listening to others and trying to discern what's true and what isn't.

RIGHTEOUSNESS

SCRIPTURE READING: 1 JOHN 2:29

Righteousness is a long word. What does it mean? Simply being or doing what's right.

There are two sides to righteousness: the *being* side and the *doing* side. Righteousness is assigned—or given—to everyone who trusts in Jesus Christ to forgive his or her sins. But God has done even more than forgiving your sins through Jesus Christ. He has also deposited righteousness into your account, like birthday money your grandparents put in your bank account. That's the *being* side.

On the *doing* side, righteousness is about more than just doing the right thing. It includes your motivation—the reasons why you do the right things and don't do the wrong things. You could do the right thing (being really nice and helpful at home) but mess it up with the wrong motivation (acting that way to avoid a punishment you deserved or to get a reward).

A teacher told a young boy to sit down. He didn't want to sit down, but he knew he would get in trouble if he didn't. So he sat down. Yet the entire time he was thinking, *I'm sitting down on the outside, but I'm standing up on the inside.* Unlike the boy's teacher, who couldn't see his heart, God sees deep within us and measures the motives behind our actions.

If you start with a righteous heart, it will overflow into your actions.

Think of a time when you did the right thing with the wrong heart. Could anyone around you tell you had the wrong motivation? Now think of a time when you did the right thing with the right heart. How did it feel? That's what it means to live righteously.

111

RIGHTEOUSNESS

SCRIPTURE READING: 1 JOHN 3:7

This week we're learning about righteousness, a major theme throughout the entire Bible. Righteousness means doing the right thing and making the right choices and decisions. To be righteous is to be without stain or blemish in character.

We know that Jesus Christ is the only example of perfect righteousness. Our goal is to be like Him. But we can never become perfectly righteous by human effort, which is why accepting the perfect work of Christ on our behalf is so important.

When we place our faith in Jesus Christ and ask Him to forgive our sins, Christ credits His perfect righteousness to us.

For today's family discussion, let's talk about the perfectly righteous character of Christ. How did Jesus Christ display perfect righteousness in His life on Earth? What kind of person was He while on Earth? In what ways can you display that same character to the world, your friends, and the members of our family?

(This discussion will help your family pursue on a day-to-day basis the perfect righteousness we've already received through faith in Christ.)

Let's close in prayer, thanking God for giving us His perfect righteousness in Christ and for helping us do what's right.

RIGHTEOUSNESS

SCRIPTURE READING: ISAIAH 33:15–17

Being right, doing right, and thinking right make the Lord happy in so many ways. This also makes the people around us feel loved and at peace and gives our hearts a spirit of peace and contentment too.

Let's spend Wednesday in the Word looking at what God says about this very long word: *righteousness.*

Little children, let no one deceive you! The one who does what is right is righteous, just as He is righteous. I JOHN 3:7
Name three things you can do that are right.

How happy are those who uphold justice, who practice righteousness at all times. PSALM 106:3
According to this verse, does doing what's right make us happy? Why or why not?

[I pray that you will be] filled with the fruit of righteousness that comes through Jesus Christ to the glory and praise of God. PHILIPPIANS 1:11
Righteousness is a fruit that Jesus Christ and the Holy Spirit give us. What is one way we can spend time with Jesus and the Spirit in our thoughts?

Anyone who lives by the truth comes to the light, so that his works may be shown to be accomplished by God. JOHN 3:21
What kinds of works do you believe God can accomplish through you?

Doing what is righteous and just is more acceptable to the LORD than sacrifice. PROVERBS 21:3
Explain the difference between doing something right and sacrificing for God. Why do you think it's more important to God that we do what's right than sacrifice?

All Scripture is inspired by God and is profitable for teaching, for rebuking, for correcting, for training in righteousness. 2 TIMOTHY 3:16
What is one way to be trained in righteousness?

RIGHTEOUSNESS

SCRIPTURE READING: PSALM 106:3

One day a little boy named Blake was trying to put a puzzle together. He tried for forty-five minutes, but he just couldn't do it. He was ready to give up when his mom asked what was wrong. Blake said he couldn't get the the puzzle pieces to fit. Blake's mom came over to help and noticed that Blake was trying to put the puzzle together without looking at the picture on the front of the box.

She explained that he must look at the picture, using it as a guide to fit the puzzle pieces together in just the right way. Blake did that, and after only ten minutes, he had completed the puzzle. He realized that constructing a perfect puzzle depends on having a perfect picture to look at.

Every person struggles with putting the right pieces of life together. We all make mistakes. We're all human. Sometimes Christians become frustrated when life just doesn't seem to be coming together; they just can't get it right. But even though none of us can put all the pieces together perfectly, Jesus Christ is the perfect picture of righteousness. He lived a perfect life without making any mistakes, so He is the perfect one to guide us when we need to put the pieces of life together. The closer we are to modeling Christ in our lives, the closer we are to living lives of righteousness.

Just for fun, let's put a puzzle together as a family. *(If you don't have a puzzle, draw and color a picture on a piece of paper; then cut it into different shapes. Or use pictures cut out from a magazine.)* Try to put the puzzle together without any picture to go by. Does it make things harder? Let's pray together and thank God that He has given us a picture of a fully complete life through His Word.

RIGHTEOUSNESS

SCRIPTURE READING: I PETER 3:14

I'm sure you've heard the saying "You are what you eat." And you know what it means. Good foods like protein, fruit, healthy fats, and vegetables build up your body and make you strong and healthy. Junk food—like candy, chips, and soda—doesn't allow your body to function at its best, and if you eat *too* much junk food, it can make you sick.

Did you know that the Bible is to the spirit what food is to the body? As the Word of God feeds your spirit, your actions will begin to naturally reflect God's viewpoint on life. You won't just react based on something you read or hear. Your life will completely change as the Holy Spirit's truth and righteousness influence you.

Eating a few grapes and a forkful of salad isn't going to instantly make you a healthier person. It takes meal after meal of eating right to get the benefits of a wholesome diet. Likewise, feeding the righteousness that God's Spirit has planted within you will take more than a minute. You need to read God's Word—the Bible—and chew on what He is saying to you. You need to think about it over and over and over again. Let God's Word and His righteousness become as real in your thoughts as the world you see around you.

For today's Fun Friday activity, let's each think of one righteous action we can do today for someone else in our home. Think of something creative. Then be sure to do it sometime today or tonight. You'll discover how much fun it is to do the right thing. You probably already do a lot of right things, but let's live intentionally and have lots of fun as we practice righteousness in our family!

INTEGRITY

SCRIPTURE READING: PROVERBS 10:9

Have you ever seen a building implode? To implode means to collapse in on itself. One second you're looking at a firmly standing building, bridge, or tunnel, and within seconds, the entire thing turns into a pile of ash and debris.

In the controlled-demolition industry, a number of small explosives are placed strategically throughout a structure. The explosives are quickly detonated within a set time frame so the structure's integrity is destroyed all at once, and the structure collapses on itself almost in a free fall.

Have you ever tried to build a house out of a deck of cards? It's easy at first. But the higher you go, the more difficult it becomes. Pretty soon just one wrong move—or one wobbly finger—and the whole thing falls down.

Let's try to build a tower as high as we can with a deck of cards. What happens if you try to remove just one card from the lower part of the tower?

Structural integrity requires piecing together different parts to build an object that will stand firm. Personal structural integrity requires that you piece together your thoughts, words, and actions in a way that will enable you to grow stronger as a person. As we saw with the stack of cards, it doesn't take much for your entire life to collapse into chaos.

The structural integrity of your life is just as important as the structural integrity of a building. What you say and do has an impact on how you live. A life built on good decisions can come crashing down in a moment with one wrong choice.

INTEGRITY

SCRIPTURE READING: PROVERBS 28:6

This week we're learning about integrity. Integrity means staying within the boundaries, even when no one is watching. For example, as your parents, we've given you rules to follow in this house. If you have integrity, you'll follow those rules even when we aren't watching you. It's okay to try hard to be successful in life and accomplish your dreams. But it's not okay to accomplish your dreams by breaking the rules.

For today's activity, each family member will take a turn sliding a quarter across the table toward the person sitting across from him or her. The goal is to play the game without breaking the integrity of the table. In other words, you want to slide the quarter as close to the edge, or boundary, of the table as possible without it falling off.

If you get the quarter within two inches of the edge without it falling off, you get one point. If the quarter hangs off the edge of the table but doesn't fall off, you get two points. If you slide the quarter too far and it breaks the integrity of the table, you lose one point.

Work hard to avoid breaking the table's integrity. The first person to get six points wins.

(This game shows that trying to win without integrity is impossible. Likewise, we can't win in life without biblical integrity.)

Can you describe what integrity means in your own words? *(Encourage everyone to respond.)*

Let's pray together and ask God to help us live with integrity.

INTEGRITY

SCRIPTURE READING: PROVERBS 11:3

God has a lot to say about integrity. Let's spend our Wednesday in the Word looking at some Scriptures on that topic.

May integrity and what is right watch over me, for I wait for You.
PSALM 25:21

Better a poor man who lives with integrity than a rich man who distorts right and wrong. PROVERBS 28:6

We are making provision for what is right, not only before the Lord but also before men. 2 CORINTHIANS 8:21

Whatever is true, whatever is honorable, whatever is just, whatever is pure, whatever is lovely, whatever is commendable—if there is any moral excellence and if there is any praise—dwell on these things.
PHILIPPIANS 4:8

Conduct yourselves honorably among the Gentiles, so that in a case where they speak against you as those who do what is evil, they will, by observing your good works, glorify God on the day of visitation. 1 PETER 2:12

[Share the gospel] with gentleness and respect, keeping your conscience clear, so that when you are accused, those who denounce your Christian life will be put to shame. 1 PETER 3:16

Spiritual integrity means "possessing a commitment to biblical truth and honesty, refusing to allow your character to be corrupted or compromised." It's about choosing thoughts, words, and actions that reflect what's right, pure, sincere, and honest.

Let's go around the room and each say or do something that models integrity. This could be as simple as giving another family member a compliment. Or it might mean talking about a time you helped someone. It might even mean walking over to the dishwasher and unloading it. It's your choice what to say or do, but it must model integrity.

INTEGRITY

SCRIPTURE READING: PROVERBS 19:1

Did you know that every sport uses boundary lines? These are lines around a field or court that show the boundaries within which the game must be played. A baseball field has foul lines. A football field has sidelines. A basketball court has baselines, and there are lane lines in track. As long as you stay within the boundaries, you're allowed to call any legal play you want to call in football. As long as you're within the boundaries, you can pass the ball to any teammate in basketball or hit the ball as far as you can hit it in baseball. As long as you're in your lane in track, you can run as fast as you want to run.

There's a lot of freedom in sports as long as you stay within the boundaries set by the rules. If you cross the boundaries, though, you get a penalty.

When you have integrity, you stay within the boundaries. When you follow the rules in the Bible, you have the chance to succeed in life. Staying within the boundaries of God's rules means living a life of integrity.

Let's do an activity that demonstrates boundaries. *(Clearly mark off two sides of the room you're in and explain the rules as follows.)* The outside of both these lines is out of bounds. *(Point out the lines.)* As long as you stay in bounds, you get to laugh, have fun, and goof around. But as soon as a I yell "Out of bounds," everyone needs to go out of bounds. When you're outside the lines, you aren't allowed to make any noises, smile, or move around. You have to be perfectly still like a statue.

(When you're finished, discuss whether family members preferred being inside or outside the boundaries.)

Did you like being inside or outside the boundaries? Why?

What are the benefits of living according to God's rules and staying within His boundaries?

This activity illustrates that we find true joy and happiness only when we're living by God's rules.

INTEGRITY

SCRIPTURE READING: PROVERBS 20:7

Remember yesterday's game? It reminded us that for true success in life, we need ethical, moral, legal, and, most importantly, biblical boundaries. These boundaries aren't to keep us from enjoying our freedom; they provide an environment where we can flourish without being penalized.

In today's world, most people define *freedom* as "a life with no boundaries." However, that's the definition of *chaos*. How can people be free to express themselves if their lives are full of chaos because of a lack of integrity?

You may be extremely talented, but if you lack the ability to showcase your gifts and talents within the boundaries, you'll never reach your full potential. Success in life depends on integrity, and integrity will always contribute to true success.

For our Fun Friday activity, let's explore boundaries. *(Go to a sink, grab a glass, and fill it with water.)* See how the boundary of the glass holds the water in place? *(Now take a drink from the glass.)* The boundary of the glass helped me drink the water, didn't it?

Now let's pour the glass of water into a bowl. It's the same water, but it doesn't have the same boundary, which makes it much harder to drink. If you try to drink it, it will probably spill. Would you like to try? *(If no one volunteers, try it yourself, exaggerating how hard it can be.)* It's very difficult to drink water neatly from a bowl because the boundary is different.

What do you think it means to follow God's boundaries and rules in our own lives? *(Encourage discussion.)*

Let's pray together and thank God for His gift of boundaries.

TRIALS

SCRIPTURE READING: ROMANS 5:3–5

Anyone who has been to school knows about tests. But few understand that, spiritually speaking, the true purpose of a test is to see what you know; if you do well, you will be rewarded. If you've completed your assignments, studied the material, and prepared properly, the result of the test is predictable: You'll receive a reward in the form of a good grade and advancement.

If you're prepared, your trials will also provide you with an opportunity to move forward in life. When trouble appears, it's as if God is saying, "Clear your desk and grab your pencil. Here comes a test." God wants to know the same thing your math teacher wants to know: Have you understood and learned the information He gave you to study?

There's no getting around it. Tests at school make people nervous. And trials cause pain. But nothing compares with the happiness you feel when you know you've done well and scored high.

Have you ever taken a test you weren't prepared for? What happened? How did you feel?

Now compare that with a test you took that you did prepare for. Were you less concerned or worried about the test you were prepared for? Why or why not?

Usually if we understand the material, we'll worry less about the test. This is because we know we can pass it.

God wants us to understand what it means to be Christlike (having a heart filled with love, kindness, forgiveness, and faith). So sometimes He'll give us a test (a trial or a difficult situation) to allow us to see how far we've come in those areas—and how far we still need to go.

View life's trials as opportunities to show God, and yourself, how deeply you trust Him!

TRIALS

SCRIPTURE READING: JAMES 1:2–4

This week we're learning about trials. Trials are the things that happen in life that make us feel sad, nervous, angry, or afraid. Trials are certain to come our way in life, but some happen because of our disobedience. They're the painful consequences of our actions and choices.

Of course, we'd all like to avoid trials! But everyone goes through hard times in life; there are no exceptions. Even Jesus Christ experienced trials. His own people rejected Him, and He died on a cross. But Jesus shows us that even though we go through hard times, they can help us become better Christians.

Have you had any sad moments recently? Has anything made you feel sad, afraid, or angry? What did you learn from that situation?

Our trials in life can end up making us stronger. God allows negative trials to create positive people. Have you ever had a bad experience that made you stronger? How did it make you stronger?

Let's pray and thank God for giving us the strength we need to get through life's trials.

TRIALS

SCRIPTURE READING: 1 PETER 4:12–13

None of us ever really wants to take a test at school, do we? And no one ever really wants to go through a challenge or a trial in life. We don't see people lining up to request one. Trials aren't fun, but God has a purpose for the pain.

Let's see what He has to say about trials in His Word.

Even when I go through the darkest valley, I fear no danger, for You are with me; Your rod and Your staff—they comfort me. PSALM 23:4

I have told you these things so that in Me you may have peace. You will have suffering in this world. Be courageous! I have conquered the world. JOHN 16:33

We also rejoice in our afflictions, because we know that affliction produces endurance. ROMANS 5:3

Rejoice in hope; be patient in affliction; be persistent in prayer. ROMANS 12:12

A man who endures trials is blessed, because when he passes the test he will receive the crown of life that God has promised to those who love Him. JAMES 1:12

Now the God of all grace, who called you to His eternal glory in Christ Jesus, will personally restore, establish, strengthen, and support you after you have suffered a little. 1 PETER 5:10

What promises does God make in the passages we just read? How does He use the challenges or struggles we face to help us grow?

The pain of a trial can be compared to the pain of lifting weights. What happens to our muscles when we lift weights? What happens to our spirits and character when we respond rightly to the trials in our lives?

TRIALS

SCRIPTURE READING: 2 CORINTHIANS 6:4–8

One day at the fair, a little boy named Kamden was excited to see balloons in the shape of different animals. He asked his parents, "Can I have one of those balloons, please?"

Soon they found a clown who was making balloon animals. Kamden asked for a bunny, and the clown went to work. He blew up several balloons. Then he twisted and turned them in different directions. Kamden covered his ears. He thought the balloons would pop because they were being stretched, pulled, and bent so much.

Kamden asked, "Why are you being so rough with those balloons?"

The clown responded, "I have to blow them up, stretch them out, bend them, and pull them to make them into the image of the rabbit you want. Without being hard on the balloons, I could never create your rabbit."

There will be times in life when you'll feel as if life's circumstances are stretching, pulling, bending, and blowing you up. But always remember, those experiences are a necessary part of being shaped into the image of Jesus Christ.

Some people say they want to be like Christ, yet in the same breath, they say they don't want to face trials. Trials, however, are always part of the process.

Let's have some fun pulling up images of balloon animals on our smartphones, computer, or tablet. *(If you don't have any electronic devices to look at, just draw some pictures that look like simple balloon animals. Or if you have time earlier, get some long balloons at a party store and let everyone make balloon animals of their own.)* Be sure to notice how many twists and turns it takes to make a recognizable animal. Everybody pick your favorite animal and tell the rest of us why it's your favorite.

TRIALS

SCRIPTURE READING: I PETER 1:6–7

God can use life's trials and challenges to strengthen us and build our character. He promises that when we love Him and live according to His purpose, He'll see that whatever we go through produces something good in our lives (see Romans 8:28). It might be difficult right now, but God will turn your trial into something worthwhile if you'll trust and honor Him through the struggle.

Remember when we talked about exercising our muscles to help them get stronger? Exercise doesn't always feel good. It can hurt. Let's see for ourselves right now! *(Note: Be careful not to push to the point of injury!)*

For our Fun Friday activity, we're going to have a sit-up contest! Let's see if everyone can do ten sit-ups, then twenty, thirty, or even fifty. The more sit-ups you do, the more you're going to feel some burning in your stomach muscles. Guess what? It's going to hurt there tomorrow as well.

Trials can be like that. They usually aren't over in a moment. They can go on and on, and the pain can linger for a while. So remember to keep your eyes on Jesus when you're in pain. He's there with you, and He's going to use your trials for good someday, somehow.

Think of it like this: A young child has an asthma attack, and his mom takes him to the doctor for a shot. The child can't understand why his mom would let him feel that pain, but it's necessary so the child can breathe freely and get better.

God doesn't always explain things to us in a way we understand in the present. Sometimes He's developing qualities in our lives that won't produce fruit for years. But we can trust that He knows what He's doing despite how things may look or feel.

Let's close in prayer, thanking God for what He's doing in our lives, and asking Him to help us trust Him when trials come our way.

SERVANTHOOD

SCRIPTURE READING: LUKE 22:27

Servanthood is a mind-set, a way of life. It isn't one act we do at one time; it's something that defines our hearts. When we have the heart of a servant, acts of service will flow naturally from our lives.

To serve means to give support or help, making it easier for someone to complete a task or enabling something to happen.

We can serve in a variety of ways, from doing something nice for someone to encouraging people with our words. Serving might be as simple as sharing your lunch with a friend or as complex as helping your teacher get the class organized at the end of the school day. It might include going on a missions trip to help those who don't have clean water or enough food.

Serving others ought to be a way of life, not an item on a to-do list. In fact, God tells us that the reason He created us was to serve. He says, "We are [God's] workmanship, created in Christ Jesus for good works, which God prepared beforehand so that we would walk in them" (Ephesians 2:10, NASB).

God created us for good works. *Good works* is another way of saying *serving others*.

Let's practice serving right now! Think of one practical way to serve another family member. You could take out the trash, pick up after a family member, fold the clothes, or read a story to a younger sibling.

Now you come up with some ideas. Serving can be really fun. Especially when you see the smile it brings to those you serve!

SERVANTHOOD

SCRIPTURE READING: PHILIPPIANS 2:7

This week we're learning about servanthood. When you demonstrate servanthood, it means that you're always looking for ways to help someone else. It's the opposite of being selfish. What is selfishness? That's when you care only about yourself and what you need.

When you have a servant's heart, you put the needs of other people first and think about yourself second. That's what Jesus Christ did: He came to serve others, laying down His life for us when He died on the cross for our sins. Because Jesus is our king and leader and we are His followers, we want to follow His example of servanthood.

In the past, have you ever been a servant? Or would you rather be served?

What are some different ways we can serve one another? What are some things we can do for people outside our family to show them the love of God?

Now let's pray, asking God to show us ways to serve others, just as His Son served us.

SERVANTHOOD

SCRIPTURE READING: JOHN 12:26

G od has made it very clear to us that He created us for service and good works, and that servanthood should be our mind-set. Let's look at what He says in Scripture about serving.

Sitting down, [Jesus] called the Twelve and said to them, "If anyone wants to be first, he must be last of all and servant of all."
MARK 9:35

Whoever wants to be first among you must be a slave to all. For even the Son of Man did not come to be served, but to serve, and to give His life—a ransom for many. MARK 10:44–45

When Jesus had washed [the disciples'] feet and put on His robe, He reclined again and said to them, "Do you know what I have done for you? You call Me Teacher and Lord. This is well said, for I am. So if I, your Lord and Teacher, have washed your feet, you also ought to wash one another's feet." JOHN 13:12–14

You were called to be free, brothers; only don't use this freedom as an opportunity for the flesh, but serve one another through love.
GALATIANS 5:13

Based on the gift each one has received, use it to serve others, as good managers of the varied grace of God. 1 PETER 4:10

According to these Bible verses, what does God say about serving others? Let's choose one or two of these verses and text them to each other or copy them down on posters and decorate them to display. This will help us remember God's important message about serving one another.

SERVANTHOOD

SCRIPTURE READING: MARK 10:42–45

Thousands of men and women in America risk their lives every day to serve our country. They leave their wives or husbands at home with their children and go to a foreign land to help other people they don't even know. The soldiers who serve our country give Americans the opportunity to experience freedom. Soldiers are the individuals who keep us safe.

When a soldier does a great job of serving, he or she will usually receive a medal. The soldier may even receive a medal from the commander in chief, the president of the United States. Medals demonstrate to soldiers how much their service is appreciated. By giving our soldiers these medals, the president recognizes the sacrifices they've made for the benefit of the entire nation.

As Christians we're called to serve the kingdom of God. Jesus said, "The greatest among you will be your servant" (Matthew 23:11). Serving the kingdom of God is a sacrifice just like the sacrifices a soldier makes for his or her country. When we serve others, we set our own needs and interests aside for the benefit of others, for their growth and freedom. When we do that, people will see Jesus Christ working through us to care for them. People can experience freedom through our service as we tell them about the Lord.

Let's take a moment to write a thank-you note to a solder or veteran who has served our nation. *(If you don't know of anyone personally, you can always ask your pastor or seek out a veteran in your church. It could be a family member as well.)* Write a sincere thank-you explaining how much you appreciate that person's service for our nation.

129

SERVANTHOOD

SCRIPTURE READING: 2 CORINTHIANS 4:5

You are here to serve and bring good to those around you—whether that's our family, your baby sister, your friends, your teachers, or people you don't know who live halfway around the world. Doing good works for God is one reason you're here on this earth, and it's why you were created in the first place.

Service isn't based on feelings. It's based on simply doing what you were put here to do. You shouldn't serve only when you feel like it. When you serve with a right attitude, you expect nothing in return. You serve so God might be glorified and others can benefit. Doing something for someone else and then expecting something in return is called business, not service. While there's nothing wrong with doing business, you need to understand the difference. It's service only when something is done to glorify God and freely help someone else.

No matter how small or how big the action, when it's accompanied by the right spirit of service, God takes notice. He has created you for a life of greatness, and that greatness comes by walking the path of service.

For our Fun Friday activity, we'll write each of our names on a piece of paper and put the names in a bowl. Then we'll pass the bowl around and let everyone draw a name. If you draw your own name, put the paper back in the bowl and draw again. Be sure not to let anyone see whose name you got. *(If any family members can't read, help them.)* This family member will be your "secret service" person. You'll do things in secret that will help him or her.

After secretly serving for a week, we'll get back together as a family and share who drew whose name. Share which secret services each family member did and how each one felt about it. Have fun serving. And serve well.

PEACE

Scripture Reading: 2 Thessalonians 3:16

It seems as if we see the word *peace* all over the place these days. The popular peace symbol decorates jewelry, bumper stickers, T-shirts, and notebooks. But peace is much more than a picture or a symbol.

In the Bible, *peace* means "completeness, wholeness, and an inner resting of the soul that never changes despite whatever else is going on." A person who is at peace is someone who is calm, untroubled, and at rest within. A person *not* at peace, of course, is filled with inner chaos, anxiety, and worry.

Did you know that you can have peace in the middle of a storm on a beach with waves crashing all around you? Or that you can have peace at school with other kids being noisy all around you? You can even have peace in the middle of a messy room. It's true. You can.

One way you can have this kind of peace is by calling on the Lord during those times and asking Him to calm your heart and mind. Another way is to look at Scripture verses when you're feeling anxious. A third way is to write out or say calming words that remind you of God's truth.

Let's write down some affirmations of peace right now. You can text them on your phone, write them on a tablet, notebook, or journal—or simply say them aloud over and over until you feel you truly know them. Here are three affirmations to get you started:

1. God will never leave me or forsake me. I'm safe and secure in His loving care.
2. God is in control of all things. When life feels out of control, I trust that He knows right where I am.
3. I love that God is bigger and stronger than any storm or problem I face.

Let's pray and thank God for His gift of peace.

PEACE

SCRIPTURE READING: PHILIPPIANS 4:6

This week we're learning about peace. Peace is something that everyone is after. People in today's world will pay a lot of money to find peace. They pay for expensive hotels and fancy vacations to put themselves in a temporary state of peace that they wish they had all the time.

The peace of God that we read about in the Bible, "surpasses all understanding" (Philippians 4:7, ESV). That means it's hard to grasp. It's totally different from the temporary peace many people are searching for. Biblical peace doesn't mean that everything is always okay, that the sun is constantly shining in our lives.

According to the Bible, the peace of God means that we're able to trust God no matter what is going on in our lives. It means that we trust Him even when life may be a struggle. We know we can rest because God will take care of us.

What does it take to have peace when everything is falling apart in your life? How can God expect this to be possible?

Have you ever been in a situation where you had peace even though you shouldn't have? Is there anything going on in your life that you're worried about? Let's pray about it right now and ask the Lord to give us all His peace even when life is hard.

We can trust that God will give us peace even in difficult times.

PEACE

SCRIPTURE READING: JOHN 16:33

For today's Wednesday in the Word, let's look at a Bible story that shows the power of God's peace in the presence of problems. When Shadrach, Meshach, and Abednego were forced to choose whether to bow down and worship King Nebuchadnezzar as god or be thrown into a fiery furnace, the three teenagers stood by their principles and refused to bow down. Here's what they said in response to the threat against them:

> *O Nebuchadnezzar, we have no need to answer you in this matter.*
> *If this be so, our God whom we serve is able to deliver us from the*
> *burning fiery furnace, and he will deliver us out of your hand,*
> *O king. But if not, be it known to you, O king, that we will not*
> *serve your gods or worship the golden image that you have set up.*
> DANIEL 3:16–18, ESV

God didn't keep the young men from the fire. In fact, they were thrown into it. Yet even though God allowed this terrible thing to happen, He didn't leave them to face it alone. He joined them in the fire!

When the king looked into the fiery furnace, he saw *four* men walking around in the midst of the fire. God didn't change their situation. Instead, He was right there with them in the middle of it.

God won't always change your situation either—though sometimes He will. But He will be right there beside you in the fiery furnace, and He'll give you the peace you need to overcome your problems when you trust Him.

Let's look up Isaiah 26:3 together. Write out the verse on a piece of paper. Make the letters into decorations and use the verse to create a beautiful picture of things that remind you of God's peace.

PEACE

SCRIPTURE READING: MATTHEW 5:9

A newly married couple went on a cruise for their honeymoon, even though the wife, Natalie, was nervous about traveling across the vast ocean. As the ship headed home at the end of the cruise, a violent storm came up. The massive waves tossed the ship around. Natalie was suddenly afraid that she and her husband, Maurice, were in serious danger.

Inside their small cabin, Natalie looked fearfully at her husband and saw that he was smiling, totally at peace. His feet were even crossed as he relaxed on the bed.

She asked, "How can you smile and be so peaceful during this terrible storm?"

Maurice said, "Didn't I tell you? My dad is the captain."

When you know that your heavenly Father is the captain of your life, you can experience a peace that surpasses understanding. You can experience peace in times that aren't peaceful at all.

Have you ever ridden in a car during a really bad storm? How did that make you feel? Can you describe the storm? Was there lightning and wind? Who was driving the car?

Did you feel safe with that person? Why or why not?

When we're driving with someone we trust, we feel safer with that person behind the wheel. Try to think about God that way too.

When life is filled with problems, remember that He is in control of this whole world, especially of your life. Trust Him, breathe deeply, and relax. He's got you!

PEACE

SCRIPTURE READING: PHILIPPIANS 4:7

Two painters were each asked to paint a picture of peace. Whoever painted the best picture would win one hundred thousand dollars. Both painters wanted to create the best possible painting to win the prize.

The first painter created a calming portrait of a lake. The sun danced across the top of the water. A small child walked near the lake holding her father's hand. Trees stood off to one side, and birds gathered in the tallest branches. Sounds peaceful, doesn't it?

The second artist had a different idea when he painted his picture. Lightning ripped across the pitch-black sky. Ocean waves churned and foamed, and trees bowed down in the wind. Does that sound peaceful?

Yet if you looked closely at the second painting, just near the very edge of this scary scene, you'd see a little bird standing on a rock. The bird had its mouth open and seemed to be singing a beautiful song. One faint ray of light shone down from the dark clouds onto the bird as it sang in spite of the storm.

The second painter won the competition. He showed what real peace looks like. Peace doesn't mean that everything is calm. When all is calm, we're supposed to feel at peace. Real peace means we're calm even when everything is falling apart.

For our Fun Friday activity, each of us will have twenty minutes to draw a picture that reflects what true peace is like. Then we'll go around the room and share what we like about each person's picture.

Before we do the activity, let's pray and thank God for His peace in the storms of life.

PERSEVERANCE

Scripture Reading: James 1:12

A story is told of a young boy who discovered a cocoon in a back-yard tree. He studied the cocoon carefully, looking for some sign of life. At last, several days later, the boy saw what he had been waiting for. Inside the filmy shell, a newly formed butterfly was struggling to get out.

Filled with compassion for the tiny creature, the boy used his pocketknife to enlarge the hole. Exhausted, the butterfly tumbled out and lay there. What the boy didn't know was that the struggle to escape was designed to strengthen the butterfly's muscle system and prepare it for flight. What he thought was an act of compassion actually crippled and ultimately doomed the butterfly to death.

Trials make us stronger. *Perseverance* is a big word that means "to keep going even when things are hard." Sometimes we want to quit when things get hard, but the effort we put in to keep going will make us stronger.

Have you ever noticed that you get stronger when you exercise regularly? Maybe you could do only ten sit-ups at first, but after a while, you could do twenty or even more. When you keep pushing yourself even though it's difficult, you grow stronger.

Okay, it's exercise time. We're all going to see how many sit-ups or push-ups we can do. Take turns and count. Do as many as you can. If you practice perseverance, sticking with the exercises instead of giving up when things get hard, you'll build up your muscles and make yourself stronger.

PERSEVERANCE

SCRIPTURE READING: ROMANS 5:3–5

Perseverance means sticking with something that becomes difficult. It's easy to give up when things get hard. For example, if you're hiking up a steep hill, halfway up you may feel like stopping or heading back down. You get tired. We all get tired. But God wants us to strengthen our physical and spiritual muscles so we'll keep going when life gets hard.

How would you respond to the following situations? *(Encourage everyone to contribute to the discussion.)*

1. Because of a job transfer to a different city, our family has to move to a new town in the middle of the school year. Even if you're homeschooled, that means leaving your friends at church or in your co-op. You aren't looking forward to this move! What are some things you can do to help yourself adjust to it?

2. At school, someone said something in front of the entire class that wasn't true about you. You didn't have the chance to defend yourself or correct what was said, and now the bell has rung. What will you do?

In life, you have to learn how to respond to hard situations without quitting. You're going to have bad days. You'll have to deal with negative people. Our family might even move to a new town or new state. We could change churches, which would mean attending a new youth group. Someone who liked you last week might say something negative about you this week. Or a class that used to be easy might be hard now because you got a new teacher. Or someone in our family will get sick or have financial problems.

Whatever the problem is—big or small—how you respond to it will determine how well you move forward in life. When something makes life hard for you, respond to it with perseverance. Remember, perseverance can be learned, but it takes practice. Let's start now!

PERSEVERANCE

SCRIPTURE READING: GALATIANS 6:9

Galatians 6:9 is probably one of the most well-known verses on perseverance. It encourages us not to give up doing good, even if we don't see the results. Let's read this passage together: "Let us not lose heart in doing good, for in due time we will reap if we do not grow weary" (NASB).

What does it mean to grow weary? Have you ever grown weary while trying to do good? For example, has your room ever been so messy that it took a really long time to clean it up? How did you feel as you kept cleaning without any end in sight? That feeling of wanting to stop or take a break is called growing weary.

But in His Word, God encourages us to keep going, because if we refuse to give in to weariness, He will reward us in "due time." Now due time doesn't necessarily mean today. It may not even mean tomorrow. But at the right time, we'll be rewarded.

Share a time when you felt like quitting but decided to keep on doing something good. What made you stick with it?

Let's look at a couple more Bible verses that talk about perseverance.

As for you . . . do not grow weary of doing good.
2 THESSALONIANS 3:13, NASB

You have need of endurance, so that when you have done the will of God, you may receive what was promised. HEBREWS 10:36, NASB

Let's close our time in prayer, asking God to give us strength and perseverance in all we do.

PERSEVERANCE

SCRIPTURE READING: 1 CHRONICLES 16:11

Why do we need perseverance? *(Allow time for discussion.)* Perseverance is critical because it makes us stronger and gives us the ability to bounce back from life's problems.

Have you ever played a video game where the character didn't jump high enough, got hit by something thrown at him, ran off the path, or fell over a cliff? If your character was fortunate enough to have more lives, he probably poofed into nothingness and then immediately reappeared, ready to play the game again.

But if your character didn't have any more lives, he just went poof. Game over.

Life isn't a video game, but how you respond to what happens in your life affects how far you can go toward reaching your dreams and goals. Success requires resilience. Resilience is like those extra lives in a video game. It gives you the ability to bounce back and start again.

Have you ever watched a team sport like football, basketball, softball, or soccer? Anytime two teams play against each other, perseverance is the key to winning. The team that faces opposition head-on, keeps going no matter what, and responds the best to whatever is thrown at them—either on offense or defense—is often the team that outplays their opponents.

Let's test our perseverance right now. We're all going to do jumping jacks until we don't feel like doing any more. Just when you feel like giving up, do twenty more! *(You can do this activity either as a group or individually. If you do it individually, you'll be able to cheer each other on. It helps to have encouragement when you need to persevere.)*

PERSEVERANCE

SCRIPTURE READING: 2 TIMOTHY 2:12

Sometimes life isn't fair. Bad things happen, and things change. People can disappoint you, and you can disappoint yourself. When that happens, follow these tips to increase your personal perseverance:

1. *Talk it out.* Find a trusted friend or relative and talk through what happened. Express how you're feeling. Discuss positive ways you can respond or gain a new perspective on the situation.

2. *Find your safe space.* Sometimes it helps to spend time in a place where you feel in control. Maybe that's your room, outdoors, in your car—wherever. Determine what your safe space is and go there to regain your perspective when life knocks you down.

3. *Do something small.* When you face a challenge, things can feel overwhelming. So set yourself up for success by doing something small that you know you can do.

4. *Exercise.* Whether it's walking, riding your bike, or doing a full workout at the gym, exercise is a great way to process stress, clear your mind, and put you in a position to handle your response to a situation.

5. *Help someone else.* One of the best ways to face life's trials is to help someone who is going through a trial of his or her own. It gets your focus off yourself and gives you a better perspective on your own struggle.

For our Fun Friday activity, let's do something active, like going for a bike ride or a jog! We'll try to push ourselves past the point where we feel like quitting. Then we'll keep on going!

GOALS

Scripture Reading: Philippians 3:13–14

Goals are like stepping-stones across a riverbed or stream. They're the steps we need to move ahead in life toward the greatest goal of all: living our lives fully for Christ. It's great to have short-term goals, small goals, long-term goals, and large—even HUGE—goals. They're what help us move forward.

Did you know that creating a picture of the future in your mind can help shape your goals? That's called having a vision. Often, things like your passion (what excites you), your gifts (what you're naturally good at doing), your past experiences, your interests, and even your personality can shape your vision.

When all of these elements join together at a certain point in your life, you start to get a better idea of why you're here on Earth, what your purpose is, and what steps you need to take to reach your goals.

Goals can be simple, such as "My goal is to help clean the kitchen every day this week." Or they can be more challenging, such as "My goal is to make an A in science class this year."

The great thing about goals is that you can make as many as you want. It's a smart idea to set goals in your life because they give you something to aim for as well as something to measure.

Let's each think of one goal to share as we close our family time today.

GOALS

SCRIPTURE READING: MATTHEW 6:33

This week we're learning about goals. To set a goal, start by thinking about what you want to do or where you want to be in the future.

For kids, setting goals often begins with the question "What do I want to be when I grow up?"

Let's go around the room and each answer that question. *(Grownups can talk about how you answered that question when you were very young.)*

When you have an idea about your future role in life, you've started the process of setting and reaching a goal. Where you see yourself in the future will contribute to the decisions you make in the present. The more excited you are about your future goals, the more passionately you'll pursue them now. Taking time to set goals and look further down the road than you can see right now is a first step toward making a dream become a reality.

What goals could you set to become a better Christian? *(Encourage responses.)*

You can set many important goals in both your Christian life and your personal life. The goal of forgiving someone, the goal of giving, and the goal of servanthood are just a few examples.

Now let's discuss setting some personal goals. Have you set any personal goals? What are they? What goals have you set recently? If you haven't set any, what's stopping you? Do you need some help getting started? What new goals do you think are important to set right now? What steps can you take to begin the process of achieving these goals?

Let's close our time in prayer, asking God to guide our steps and the goals we set as we think about the future He desires for each of us.

GOALS

SCRIPTURE READING: PHILIPPIANS 4:13

God's Word gives us real insight into the importance of setting goals and encourages us to stick to them. A word often used in the Bible to describe or define goals is *plans*. For today's Wednesday in the Word, let's dive right in and see what our Lord has to say.

As for you, be strong; don't be discouraged, for your work has a reward.   2 CHRONICLES 15:7

The plans of the diligent certainly lead to profit, but anyone who is reckless certainly becomes poor.   PROVERBS 21:5

Which of you, wanting to build a tower, doesn't first sit down and calculate the cost to see if he has enough to complete it?   LUKE 14:28

Whether we are at home or away [from the Lord], we make it our aim to be pleasing to Him.   2 CORINTHIANS 5:9

I pursue as my goal the prize promised by God's heavenly call in Christ Jesus.   PHILIPPIANS 3:14

According to 2 Corinthians 5:9, what should be one of our highest goals in life? What are some ways we can please God in our thoughts? What are some ways we can please God in our words? What are some ways we can please God in our actions?

Do you ever become discouraged when you're working toward a goal but find it's taking a long time? Remember that God's Word encourages you to be strong and not to be discouraged. You'll get there. And God will reward you for doing well.

GOALS

SCRIPTURE READING: 1 CORINTHIANS 9:24–27

The bald eagle is one of the most majestic birds in the world, and it's known for its keen eyesight. When it's time for the eagle to find a meal, it takes off from its nest and flies high over the ground searching for its prey.

Why does the bald eagle search for prey while it's flying so high? Because mice, snakes, and other prey can't see it circling in the sky. They have no clue they're being watched. The bald eagle can spot small animals from thousands of feet in the air and track them while it's flying.

When the bald eagle spots its next meal, it locks in on its prey with its keen eyes. Then the majestic eagle swoops down from the air quietly and swiftly and grabs its prey with its huge claws. It holds on tightly because it doesn't want to risk losing its next meal. Finally the eagle carries its prey back to its nest and eats what it first spotted only from a vast distance.

Setting goals for yourself is like an eagle hunting for its next meal. You need a keen focus on what you want to accomplish in the future. Just as an eagle must see its prey before catching it, you must first see what you want in life before you can go after it.

Let's each write down three goals or visions we want to accomplish. The first goal should be something short term that can be achieved within the next three months. The next one should be something you want to accomplish over the next year. And the third goal should be achieved within the next five years. Always remember to write down your goals! It helps you accomplish them when you see them on paper.

Let's pray and ask God to show us how to set goals that reflect the vision He has for our lives.

GOALS

Scripture Reading: Proverbs 21:5

Let's talk about a helpful tool to use as you set goals for your life. To make sure the goals you're setting are realistic and that you'll be able to reach them, remember this helpful acronym: SMART.

S— Goals need to be *specific*. This will help you make choices about what to do or not do to reach them.

M—Goals need to be *measurable* in some form or fashion.

A— Goals need to be *attainable*. For example, don't aim too high so that you wind up disappointed because your goal was unrealistic.

R— Goals need to be *relevant*, meaning they should tie in to your personal interests or needs; otherwise, you may lose interest over time.

T— Goals need to have a *time frame* associated with them. This will help you stay on track as you pursue your goals and not leave you prone to procrastination.

Now that we've looked at how to assess some of our goals, let's talk about the difference between a long-term goal and a short-term goal. A long-term goal might be losing twenty pounds in one year to reach what the doctor recommends as a healthy weight. A short-term goal might be to lose two pounds in a month, or even to eat healthy today. What are some other examples?

For today's activity, let's all write down one long-term goal and one short-term goal we'd like to accomplish as a family. These are different from the goals we wrote down yesterday. We can never have too many goals. We'll post these goals on the refrigerator or someplace prominent so we're reminded to ask one another how we're doing as we work on these goals.

TEAMWORK

SCRIPTURE READING: ECCLESIASTES 4:9–12

E veryone has heard the phrase "There's no *I* in team." In team sports, no one can determine the outcome of a game apart from his or her teammates.

It's true in sports, and it's true in life: We need to have unity as a team. But don't forget this very important point: Unity does *not* mean uniformity. It doesn't mean that everyone is alike.

Think about your favorite team or band. What if everyone on that team played the same position? It wouldn't be a winning team! What if every band member played the same instrument or the same notes? That band wouldn't make any music worth listening to.

The definition of *unity* is "working together toward a shared purpose." It isn't being exactly the same in everything we do as a team.

So be unique! Be an individual! Work as a team by contributing your special skills and abilities to the overall goal of advancing God's kingdom.

To illustrate the importance of being different while playing on the same team, we're going to play a game called Pictionary. First, we'll need to divide up into two teams. *(Make it an even number, if possible. If you only have three people, take turns having one person draw while the other two guess.)* One team member will choose a popular movie, book, sports team, or location and draw pictures representing it on a piece of paper without speaking. Other team members will try to guess what is being drawn. Each team will take turns, and we'll play until one team gets to five.

(After the game, ask the following question.) What would have happened if everyone on your team drew pictures but nobody guessed? *(Encourage discussion. The obvious answer is "You wouldn't have scored any points.")*

Being on the same team doesn't mean that everyone does the same thing. It means working toward the same goal.

TEAMWORK

SCRIPTURE READING: PROVERBS 27:17

This week we're learning about teamwork. Teamwork means working together with other people to achieve a common goal. This is most often seen in team sports. What team sports can you name? What would happen if someone tried to play a team sport all alone?

The Christian life is like a team sport. It isn't meant to be lived alone. You must have people in your life who are on your team. That means they share the same goal and purpose and are going in the same direction. Who's on your team?

Brothers and sisters in Christ are our team members. We're meant to grow into the image of Jesus Christ together. This team is called the *body of Christ*. It includes a variety of people brought together to serve one purpose—to grow into the image of Christ. Having a team of Christians in your life is just as important as having a team in sports.

Let's play a game that will help illustrate this idea. *(Get a small, soft ball that you can toss around.)* The goal of the game is to toss a ball across the room ten times without dropping it once. If anyone on the team drops the ball, then we have to start over.

Now think about the people in your life who are on your team. They are there to support you and encourage you to grow in your faith. They'll "catch the ball" when you throw it to them. But if no one is there when you throw the ball, it's sure to drop. Let's not drop the ball in life simply because we don't have a team to throw to.

As we close in prayer, let's ask God to help us see our brothers and sisters in Christ as team members who are there for us and do their best not to let us down.

TEAMWORK

SCRIPTURE READING: 1 CORINTHIANS 12:20–25

God has a heart of unity. His very nature reflects the unity of the Father, the Son, and the Holy Spirit. This is one reason He longs for us to live in unity with one another.

God's Word teaches us about unity and the power of teamwork. Let's take a look at some of those verses.

> *Iron sharpens iron, and one man sharpens another.* PROVERBS 27:17

> *Two are better than one because they have a good reward for their efforts. For if either falls, his companion can lift him up; but pity the one who falls without another to lift him up.* ECCLESIASTES 4:9–10

> *I urge you, brothers, in the name of our Lord Jesus Christ, that all of you agree in what you say, that there be no divisions among you, and that you be united with the same understanding and the same conviction.* 1 CORINTHIANS 1:10

> *If the whole body were an eye, where would the hearing be? If the whole body were an ear, where would the sense of smell be?*
> 1 CORINTHIANS 12:17

> *From [Christ] the whole body, fitted and knit together by every supporting ligament, promotes the growth of the body for building up itself in love by the proper working of each individual part.*
> EPHESIANS 4:16

First Corinthians 12:17 is a great illustration of the difference between unity and uniformity. Unity doesn't mean we're all exactly alike, doing the same thing.

Imagine if your body was made up of a bunch of eyeballs or ears. That wouldn't be much of a body; that would be a freak show. For your body to work well, it requires many parts functioning together as one. That's unity!

Be sure to keep your uniqueness, but join your uniqueness with the uniqueness of others to make up a winning team.

TEAMWORK

SCRIPTURE READING: EPHESIANS 4:16

We can learn a lot about teamwork from some very common birds—geese. For instance,

As each goose flaps its wings, it creates an "uplift" for the bird following. By flying in a "V" formation, the whole flock adds 71% more flying range than if each bird flew alone. [In other words, geese flying together can travel a whole lot farther than a goose flying by itself.] *Lesson: People who share a common direction and sense of community can get where they are going quicker and easier because they are traveling on the [uplift] of one another.*

Whenever a goose falls out of formation, it suddenly feels the drag and resistance of trying to fly alone, and quickly gets back into formation to take advantage of the "lifting power" of the bird immediately in front. *Lesson: If we have as much sense as a goose, we will [stay in formation] with those who are headed where we want to go.*

When the lead goose gets tired, it rotates back into the formation and another goose flies at the point position. *Lesson: It pays to take turns doing the hard tasks and sharing leadership [being interdependent rather than independent]. . . .*

When a goose gets sick or wounded . . . , two geese drop out of formation and follow their fellow member down [to the ground] to help provide protection. They stay with this member of the flock until [it's] able to fly again. . . . Then they launch out on their own, with another formation [of geese], or catch up with their own flock. *Lesson: If we have as much sense as the geese, we'll stand by each other like that.**

Let's each draw a picture of geese flying in a "V" formation and share one way we can build teamwork by imitating their example.

---

* Dr. Robert McNeish, "Lessons from the Geese," Baltimore, Maryland, 1972, http://aikentdc
.org/Lessons_From_The_Geese.pdf.

TEAMWORK

SCRIPTURE READING: HEBREWS 10:24

For Fun Friday, we're going to play some games to help us learn this important concept of teamwork.

First, stand next to another family member and use something loose to tie your hand to the person next to you at the wrist. When finished, we'll all be tied together as a group. Then we'll choose a task to do together. Possibilities include making a sandwich, rearranging the furniture in a room, or wrapping a present. In the process we'll discover how each of us is part of a larger group of people who must come together to accomplish a goal.

Our next activity is known as Magic Shoes. In the center of the group is an area called the pond. The only way each person can get across the pond is to use a pair of magic shoes. When the leader taps someone's shoes, they become the magic shoes. Here are the rules:

1. Each family member can wear magic shoes only once.
2. When the wearer of the magic shoes wants to, he or she will tap someone else and give that person the magic shoes.
3. You cannot tap shoes that are across the pond.
4. Everyone must somehow make it across the pond.

(After you're finished playing the game, talk about the importance of working together as a team. Discuss the following questions.)

What made it easier to work together as a team? What made it more difficult?

Let's go around the room and each share how we can apply these lessons in everyday life, especially in our home. Then we'll close in prayer, asking God to help us work together as a family.

PRIORITIES

SCRIPTURE READING: MATTHEW 6:33

Priorities. That's a big word for the things that come first or matter most in our lives. For example, is it a priority to watch your favorite TV show or to do your homework the night before it's due?

If you answered that your TV show is a priority, you're actually talking about what you *want* to do, not what you *should* do. A priority is something that should come first even if you don't feel like doing it.

Setting priorities in life helps us stay on track to accomplish goals. Over and over in Scripture, we read about God asking us to make Him a priority in our lives. In fact, He tells us to put Him first. First is the most important priority.

In the book of Revelation, when Jesus scolded the church at Ephesus, He wasn't saying that the people didn't love Him at all. In fact, He applauded them, saying, "You have perseverance and have endured for My name's sake, and have not grown weary" (Revelation 2:3, NASB).

However, they had left their "first love." They no longer regarded Jesus as first in their hearts or their lives. He wasn't their top priority. What they *did* for Him was the priority, not their love for Him.

Let's each list our top five priorities on a piece of paper. Then we'll compare notes.

Do the priorities you listed reflect the way you really spend your time? Sometimes we may not realize what our priorities actually are, but what we do with our time often reveals the true picture.

Does God show up anywhere in your priorities? If He doesn't, how can you start putting Him first in your life?

PRIORITIES

SCRIPTURE READING: ROMANS 12:2

This week we're learning about priorities. When you prioritize, you list things in order from the most important to the least important. Once you identify the most important things in your life, as well as the least important things, you can live your life with your priorities in order.

For example, God is the most important person in our lives, so we want to make sure to keep Him first in everything we do. The next important priority under God should be our family. This means we should make sure we love our family members and are committed to them every day.

Write those two priorities down on a piece of paper and then think of three more priorities that would come under God and family. Let's spend some time talking about our priorities and how we can put them into action every day.

We'll close in prayer, asking God to guide us as we choose our priorities and live each day according to His calling.

PRIORITIES

SCRIPTURE READING: LUKE 12:34

If we lose sight of God and His kingdom in our priorities and fail to put Him first, we lose His perspective when we're choosing what to do with our time, talents, and treasures. We start focusing on physical and material things in life, letting them direct our emotions and choices.

When that happens, our thoughts get mixed up, and our decisions become shortsighted. Rather than living out our destiny and purpose in life, we end up wasting time, effort, energy, and emotions.

But when we put God first, giving Him our energy, thoughts, time, and emotions, we get to see heaven both rule and overrule in our lives. And we get to experience Him at a whole other level—as king.

Here's what God says in His Word about putting Him first:

Commit your activities to the LORD, and your plans will be achieved. PROVERBS 16:3

Seek first the kingdom of God and His righteousness, and all these things will be provided for you. MATTHEW 6:33

[Jesus] said to [the expert in the law], "Love the Lord your God with all your heart, with all your soul, and with all your mind." MATTHEW 22:37

[Jesus] is also the head of the body, the church; He is the beginning, the firstborn from the dead, so that He might come to have first place in everything. COLOSSIANS 1:18

Let's each take a turn reading these verses once out loud. *(If a family member can't read, have him or her repeat a verse after someone else says it.)* It's good to read God's Word aloud because it helps us remember it and apply it to our lives (which means doing what it says).

PRIORITIES

SCRIPTURE READING: DEUTERONOMY 6:5

Priorities show up in all we do, including how we handle our money. Do you spend your money, save it, or give it away? Today's activities will help us discover how we prioritize our money. Understanding this will help us make wiser decisions. *(If your children get an allowance, these activities will work in this scenario as well.)*

You'll use your imagination for the first activity, and you'll use the money you actually have for the second activity. The third activity will help us talk about the place of God and money in our lives in more detail.

1. Imagine that you make a thousand dollars a month. Create a budget covering all your required expenses. We can work on it together to figure out the right amount to spend on things like a house or apartment payment, electricity, water, a car, gas for the car, food, health care, and, above all, giving to the Lord.

2. Practice budgeting your money using a sixty-day, cash-only, envelope-based budget system. This will help reinforce the value of money as you see where and how your money is spent. Write on the envelopes the different categories that show where you plan to spend your money. Based on your past spending habits and your budget, put in each envelope the amount of cash you decided you could spend during this period of time. When the envelope is empty, refrain from spending in that area until you're able to fill the envelope again.

3. Now let's talk about putting God first in all areas of our lives, including how we spend our money. *(Encourage discussion and be prepared to offer examples.)* Why do you think God wants to be first in our lives? How does it benefit us to keep Him first? Write down (or share) two ways you're going to put God first in situations where you haven't normally done so in the past.

Let's pray together and ask God to guide our spending and put our priorities in the right order.

PRIORITIES

SCRIPTURE READING: MATTHEW 6:24

We've been talking about priorities this week and why it's important to always keep God first. Keeping God first doesn't mean just going to church on Sunday or spending time talking with Him at a certain time each day. It means making sure He is an active part of your life, thoughts, and actions all throughout the day.

For example, if God chose to give us oxygen only on Sundays or for five minutes each day, would He be putting our lives first? Not really. We need oxygen all the time to live. Similarly, for God to have the priority He should have in our lives, we need to put Him first in all of our thoughts throughout the day. While we won't do this perfectly, the Holy Spirit can help us if we ask Him.

For our Fun Friday activity, let's think of some practical ways we can put God first. As we go around the room, each of us will share one idea. Then we'll go around two more times! We should have lots of ideas when we're finished.

For the next activity, we'll discuss what could happen in different situations if we don't put God first in our thoughts or actions. What if someone cut in front of you in line? Or what if you were on the computer and were tempted to look at or click on something you shouldn't? How might not putting God first change the outcome of each situation?

Let's close in prayer, asking God to continue leading us and directing our priorities each day.

HARD WORK

SCRIPTURE READING: COLOSSIANS 3:23

You may not always understand why you need to do your chores or complete your homework. But as you grow older, hard work will often set you apart from other students or employees. The virtue of hard work will also come in handy once you have your own family and home!

This doesn't mean you should never rest or play! Remember, God worked for six days and then rested on the seventh. Balance is important. But it's easy to lean too far toward the side of rest and play and not far enough toward the side of hard work. Work hard, whether in school, at home, or in sports, and you'll receive the fruit of your labor in due time. Frequently those around you will notice, and you'll be rewarded. You'll set yourself apart as someone who goes the extra mile and takes responsibility to finish what you start.

Let's go over our regular chores. *(Make a list of the family responsibilities for each person.)* You may think you work hard at these chores, and that's great. But to practice this skill, we're going to try something that may be new to you. Think of some ways you can do more than just your chores.

What extra things can you do to help out either at home or at school? It might be dusting or emptying the trash twice a week instead of once. What can you add to your regular responsibilities? *(Once you agree on two or three things to add, write them down.)* These aren't chores. You aren't expected to do them, but when you do, you'll feel a sense of accomplishment in working hard even when you aren't required to!

HARD WORK

SCRIPTURE READING: PROVERBS 13:4

This week we're talking about hard work. When you work hard, you give your best effort every time you have an opportunity—whether it's at school, in sports and other activities, or even in your relationships with God and others. Whenever you're willing to work hard, you put yourself in a position to experience growth and success in any area of your life.

Hard work is essential to success. Everyone has God-given talent that gives them an opportunity to have a successful life. However, talent never works when hard work isn't connected to it. For your God-given talent to be displayed in your life, you must be willing to work hard. Often what God has for you is within your reach but not in your hands. That is, you have to be willing to go get it to have it.

In what areas of your life do you work hard? In what areas of your life could you work harder?

It's time to work hard in every area of our lives to maximize our God-given potential.

Let's pray and thank God for the way He has designed us to benefit from hard work. And let's ask Him for the ideas and energy we need to work and achieve all that He wants for us.

HARD WORK

SCRIPTURE READING: 2 THESSALONIANS 3:10–12

D o you think God has anything to say about hard work? Let's see
what His Word tells us.

The slacker craves, yet has nothing, but the diligent is fully satisfied.
PROVERBS 13:4

There is profit in all hard work, but endless talk leads only to
poverty. PROVERBS 14:23

Whatever your hands find to do, do with all your strength.
ECCLESIASTES 9:10

Whatever you do, do it enthusiastically, as something done for the
Lord and not for men. COLOSSIANS 3:23

When we were with you, this is what we commanded you: "If anyone
isn't willing to work, he should not eat." For we hear that there are
some among you who walk irresponsibly, not working at all, but
interfering with the work of others. Now we command and exhort
such people by the Lord Jesus Christ that quietly working, they may
eat their own food. Brothers, do not grow weary in doing good.
2 THESSALONIANS 3:10–13

God makes it clear that hard work leads to gain and reward (spiritual, material, or both), while laziness leads to loss and poverty. Can
you think of a time in your life when you chose to work hard and saw
a positive result? What happened?

Other people may not see what you do, but you can rest assured
that when you work hard for God, He always sees it, and He'll reward
you.

HARD WORK

SCRIPTURE READING: PROVERBS 14:23

Most sports fans sit in front of their TVs to watch a football game without understanding the effort the players must put in before the game even starts. A week full of practices, meetings about game plans, and watching and studying game films leaves them tired mentally, emotionally, and physically. Playing in a professional football league takes discipline, consistency, and constant hard work. The few hours spent playing the game represent only a small part of the work required. The game itself is a celebration of all the effort that came before.

Make no mistake about it, living the Christian life is also hard work. Some people think that all they have to do is sit in a pew on Sunday for an hour or so. Instead, a weekly worship service should be a collective celebration of the hard work we've done Monday through Saturday building our relationship with God.

Consistently meeting with God in devotions, taking what we've learned and living it out, and understanding how the Enemy works all contribute to being a prepared Christian. Being a Christ follower doesn't simply require one or two hours on Sunday. It demands dedication and hard work *every* day.

Do you think the Christian life is hard work? Maybe not if you look at it simply as going to church or reading your Bible. But God wants us to work hard to be better people, to serve others, and also to spend time with Him.

List three ways you can work harder in those areas this week. Then be sure to put them into practice until they become a habit in your life.

HARD WORK

SCRIPTURE READING: PROVERBS 16:3

For today's Fun Friday activity, we're going to put you in charge of dinner! It might not be tonight, but your challenge is to make dinner one night this week. That includes some planning and some work! Here are the tasks you'll need to complete:

1. Pick the meal (that includes two sides and a dessert).
2. Look up the recipes.
3. Write down the ingredients.
4. Look through the kitchen to discover what ingredients we already have. Make a list of the ingredients you need to buy.
5. Go to the store and buy the ingredients.
6. Prepare the meal and set the table.
7. Serve the meal.
8. Clean up after the meal.

Making a meal is a lot of hard work, isn't it? But this is only one small aspect of everyday life. So get used to hard work. It's required in life, and it will take you far if you learn its value early on!

COMMUNICATION

SCRIPTURE READING: JAMES 1:19

Have you ever talked to someone and felt you weren't being heard? You saw the person's eyes glaze over as his or her mind wandered off. Or when you were done talking, the person immediately changed the subject. Maybe the person clearly disagreed with you. How did you feel when that happened? It hurt, didn't it?

Disagreements are no fun, but they happen in life. Problems come when disagreements lead to hurt feelings, misunderstandings, or a break in the relationship. So let's talk about how to really hear someone you don't agree with, and how to help that person hear you.

When we disagree with people, it's important to first make sure they know that we heard what they said. You can say something as simple as "I hear that you said _____ *(fill in the blank with what that person said)*, and that makes you feel _____ *(try to guess: upset, sad, etc.)*. I can understand that."

When you say that, it lets the other person know you truly listened. That way when you disagree, it doesn't seem as if you're trying to prove your point, bully to get your way, or win an argument. After all, the goal is to come to some kind of agreement.

After you repeat what you heard the other person say, say what you think. If the other person tries to interrupt you, explain that he or she should do the same for you, since you listened nicely.

Let's try practicing this right now as a family. Surely we can find something we disagree on. Maybe one of you likes brussels sprouts and one doesn't. Take turns listening to each other and then expressing your own opinion.

Let's pray together and ask God to help us learn to be better communicators.

COMMUNICATION

SCRIPTURE READING: EPHESIANS 4:29

This week we're learning about the importance of communication. Through communication we express our thoughts and feelings to one another. We can communicate by talking or even without words.

We all can become better communicators. We want to be clear and correct so we share the right message and others receive it the way we intend. We want to be respectful to God and to others in our communication.

Let's talk about how we can do a better job communicating, whether we use words (which is verbal communication) or facial expressions and gestures (which is nonverbal communication). How can we each do a better job of *verbally* communicating our wants, needs, and expectations?

Let's practice right now! Each of us will take a turn making a facial expression while the rest of us try to guess how that person feels or figure out what he or she is trying to communicate.

For another activity, I'll think of a few words to whisper to one of you to get things started. The goal is for everyone to whisper the message around the room and see if it comes back to me in exactly the same words. This activity will help make us aware of the need to communicate better as a family.

COMMUNICATION

SCRIPTURE READING: 2 TIMOTHY 2:16

God's Word speaks to the issue of communication by teaching us to watch our mouths and use our words for good. Let's look at a few verses.

> *They make a lot of sense, these wise [people]; whenever they speak, their reputation increases.* PROVERBS 16:23, MSG

> *The right word at the right time is like a custom-made piece of jewelry.* PROVERBS 25:11, MSG

> *Watch the way you talk. Let nothing foul or dirty come out of your mouth. Say only what helps, each word a gift.* EPHESIANS 4:29, MSG

Keep in mind that communicating involves more than just words. It includes nonverbal communication and listening without using words. Can you think of an example of that?

Did you know that most of our communication is actually nonverbal? That means we're talking without actually talking. We're communicating through our gestures and posture, as well as the way we walk, sit, stand, what we wear, and whether we look people in the eyes or not—any number of ways.

Problems arise when we don't pay attention to both our verbal and nonverbal communication. Make sure to pay attention to what you're saying, even when you aren't saying anything at all.

A critical part of communication involves listening. To listen is to hear what someone has said and seek to understand it.

When you use all three communication skills—verbal communication, nonverbal communication, and listening—you have an opportunity to truly express what you want to, to be heard, and to understand what the other person is saying. If communication is one-sided, you haven't communicated successfully at all.

COMMUNICATION

SCRIPTURE READING: PROVERBS 16:23

A family was on vacation at a theme park. As a teenager, big sister Tina was reluctant to be away from her friends for a weekend. She shuffled along behind her family as they navigated through the park. Little brother Tim ran up a ramp as he raced to the mega roller coaster. Mom chased frantically after him while yelling back to Dad to hurry up. Dad was worried about Tina. She'd been distant, refusing to walk with the family, taking picture after picture and texting away on her phone.

As the day progressed, Tina seemed even more disengaged. Later, when the family returned to the hotel and everyone was getting ready for bed, Tina offered to share a video. It was a slide show of the day, complete with pictures, smiles, jokes, sound bites, and songs. It appeared that Tina hadn't been disengaged after all. In fact, she was fully engaged, but in her own way. She even posted the day's adventures on Facebook and Twitter. In her mind she was engaged; to her parents she didn't look as if she was enjoying the day at all. What do you make of this? Let's discuss it.

- Would you say that young people are more likely to be disengaged when cell phones and social media are distracting them?
- Was it a good thing or bad thing that Tina experienced her vacation differently?
- Would you say overall that she enjoyed herself? Why or why not?
- On scale of 1 to 10 (1 for low and 10 for high), how important is verbal communication?
- What are some ways social media keeps young people from being engaged with others?
- How can we set boundaries to make sure that social media doesn't prevent our family from having healthy relationships with one another?

COMMUNICATION

SCRIPTURE READING: PSALM 19:14

Communication is key, but as we've been learning, it involves a whole lot more than words. But when communication does involve words, it's important to choose our words wisely, based on what's best in the situation.

For today's Fun Friday activity, we'll all form one big human knot. You can't speak at all during this activity. *(Have everyone stand in a circle and put his or her right hand in the middle of the circle. Instruct each person to grab the right hand of someone who isn't standing next to him or her. Once this is accomplished, have everyone do the same thing with their left hands. Explain that they cannot grab the left hand of someone whose right hand they already grabbed.)*

(Afterward, discuss the following questions.) What did this activity show us about the importance of words and actions in communication? How can communication go wrong or be misunderstood, especially over social media or through text messages?

Now let's brainstorm together and make a list of topics we all like to talk about or see discussed on social media—everything from friendships to family life to daily activities.

(After you've collected an extensive list, decide which topics you'd normally share on social media. Write them on a T-shirt with a permanent marker. List the remaining topics on small pieces of paper and place the papers in a jar. When the activity is over, have someone wear the shirt.)

What do you think was the point of this activity? *(Allow time for discussion.)*

It's important to understand that social media is public and permanent. Everyone will know and always have access to the information you share online, but choosing to keep some things private—like the papers in the jar—is wise.

WORSHIP

SCRIPTURE READING: JOHN 4:24

Did you know that worship isn't only for God? When we worship God, it brings Him pleasure and delight, but it also does something for us. There are benefits that come from being in God's presence through worship. Psalm 16:11 tells us, "You reveal the path of life to me; in Your presence is abundant joy; in Your right hand are eternal pleasures." The psalmist said that worship brings joy. Being in God's presence lifts us up emotionally.

The reason King David ran to worship is that he knew where the joy was. In God's presence is "abundant joy." So if you want to be lifted up in your spirit and emotions, go to God. Sing to Him. Say nice things about Him. Tell God you love Him. You don't find joy by looking for it. You find it by being in an environment of joy. God lives in an atmosphere of joy.

You can't live in the atmosphere of the sun and not be hot. You can't live in the atmosphere of the North Pole and not get chilly. And you can't live in the atmosphere of God and not have joy.

Worship isn't something we do because we feel like it. It's something we do because God deserves it. That's why we worship.

Let's pick two or three of our favorite worship songs or hymns and sing them right now. *(You may want to pull them up online or play them from your music player.)* Be sure to join in. Singing together is an awesome thing to do, and it puts a smile on God's face and in His heart.

WORSHIP

SCRIPTURE READING: ROMANS 12:1

This week we're devoting our time to worship. We can worship God in different ways. Sometimes we might sit quietly and think about His greatness. Other times we might worship with others at church, singing and praising Him.

Often when we pray, we spend most of our time asking God to do things for us. Real worship requires us to put the focus on God and not ourselves.

Let's go around the room right now and each share some great things about God. What great things has God done for you? If you can voice these things out loud, then you can also sit quietly and tell them to God. When you do that, you're worshipping.

For today's activity, we'll spend time in worship. We'll each sit quietly with God and think about His goodness and the great things He has done. Let's take five minutes for each of us to find a quiet place in the house. *(If your kids are very young, go with them.)* Sit with the Lord for five minutes and tell Him how great He is. Thank Him for all He has done.

Worship is about God, not about us. This means it isn't a time to make requests. It's simply a time to honor God. So let's honor him together. When we're finished worshipping individually, let's come back together and worship God in prayer as a family.

WORSHIP

SCRIPTURE READING: JOHN 4:23

You don't have to look hard in Scripture to find out what God has to say about the very important topic of worship. Worship makes Him happy because He deserves our admiration and our love. It's one way of expressing those things to Him.

For today's Wednesday in the Word, let's look at the Lord's view of worship.

> *Come, let us worship and bow down; let us kneel before the LORD our Maker.* PSALM 95:6

> *Sing to Yahweh, for He has done glorious things. Let this be known throughout the earth.* ISAIAH 12:5

> *Jesus answered [the Devil], "It is written: Worship the Lord your God, and serve Him only."* LUKE 4:8

> *God is spirit, and those who worship Him must worship in spirit and truth.* JOHN 4:24

> *By the mercies of God, I urge you to present your bodies as a living sacrifice, holy and pleasing to God; this is your spiritual worship.* ROMANS 12:1

> *Since we are receiving a kingdom that cannot be shaken, let us hold on to grace. By it, we may serve God acceptably, with reverence and awe.* HEBREWS 12:28

These are just a few of the Bible verses on worship. There are so many more. But we can tell by looking at them that the Lord values and asks for our worship. We can worship Him in any number of ways. Singing is one way.

Why don't we pick a favorite worship song right now and sing it together?

WORSHIP

Scripture Reading: Luke 4:8

Walt Disney's film *The Lion King* is one of the most highly rated Disney films of all time. The story follows a lion cub named Simba who grows up to become king over the Pride Lands. At the start of his journey, he was rejected by those who should have accepted him. He was forced to travel far away, but eventually he returned to claim his place as king, an inheritance from his father. Once he took his rightful place, all the animals came to worship him and bow down before him. Even the grass began to grow and the trees began to wave in recognition of Simba as the king. At the end of the movie, all of the land and the animals pay homage to their king.*

We have a king, and His name is Jesus Christ. When He was on Earth, His people rejected Him and put Him on a cross. He has gone back to heaven for a while but will return again someday. When He returns, He will take His rightful place as the king of this world—the inheritance God the Father gave Him before time began. If the animals in *The Lion King* knew how to worship Simba, then the people of God's kingdom should know how to worship Jesus.

Let's bow our heads together right now and spend a moment honoring and worshipping our Lord. It's okay if we don't say anything at all. Sometimes it's good just to give Him our time and attention in a moment of silent worship. After a while we'll go around the room and each say something we love about Jesus. Speaking words of praise is also a form of worship.

---

* *The Lion King*, directed by Roger Allers and Rob Minkoff (Burbank, CA: Walt Disney Pictures, 1994).

WORSHIP

SCRIPTURE READING: HEBREWS 12:28

Psalm 68:4 says, "Sing to God! Sing praises to His name. Exalt Him who rides on the clouds—His name is Yahweh—and rejoice before Him." In other words, the psalmist tells us to get our praise on. Then he explains why we should praise.

Let's read Psalm 68 together. We can take turns reading one verse aloud each until we've read through the chapter. *(If anyone is unable to read, choose someone else to read the verse and then have that family member repeat the words.)*

What are some of the promises in this psalm? God says that if you're lonely, He can make a home for you. If you're locked up, God can lead you out of prison into prosperity. If you need a change of weather, like Elijah did, God can bring plenty of rain.

If you're burdened, you can read in verse 19 that the Lord "daily bears our burden" (NASB). If you need deliverance, verse 20 says that God is able to deliver you. He's the one who can help you escape. And where did the psalmist end up? Right back where he started: telling you to get your praise on (verse 35).

Whenever we march into the sanctuary, we can bless God in the congregation, because our God makes us strong. We can bless Him no matter where we are.

For today's Fun Friday activity, let's write a praise song to God. We can do it together, or you can create your own song. Come up with a simple tune and write the verses you want to sing to God. Once we've finished writing our songs, we can record them on our smartphones or tablets so we can remember them and sing them whenever we want to praise the Lord. We can even share them with our friends and other family members.

CHURCH

SCRIPTURE READING: EPHESIANS 2:20–22

Have you ever stopped to think about how truly amazing and unique the church is? It has stood the test of time! History shows us there is nothing like the church when it comes to endurance.

The Macedonian king Alexander the Great conquered the world, but within a few years of his death, his kingdom was split among four of his generals. Centuries after Alexander's death, the Roman Empire conquered the world, yet even though it lasted several hundred years, only ancient ruins and history lessons exist today.

After thousands of years, the church is still seeking, however imperfectly, to obey the purpose for which our founder, Jesus Christ, established it. The purpose of the church is to be the completion of Jesus' life and work on Earth.

Our Lord called out a people to complete the work He began. Now that Jesus is no longer among us physically, the church is meant to be His body on Earth. We're to be the hands and feet of Jesus. That means we're to do the things He would have done if He were still here, things like loving others, helping others, telling others about Jesus, restoring hope, being kind, and bringing healing and light into a darkened world.

The church also provides a place for fellowship and learning, along with worship in God's presence. That's a lot for a church to do!

Let's talk about some of the things our church is doing as Jesus' hands and feet. Then we'll each make a list of things we'd like to see our church doing even more. Maybe we could encourage people at church to start doing these things as well.

CHURCH

SCRIPTURE READING: ACTS 20:28

Some people think the church is the building they go to on Sunday to learn about God with other people. However, the church is actually the people who are in the building. It's the body of believers who have been grafted into the family tree of Abraham.

When you accept Jesus Christ as your personal savior, you immediately become part of something bigger called the body of Christ—the church. In other words, everyone who has been brought into this family through faith is part of the church.

Going to church isn't going to a building, because the church isn't a building. The building simply opens its doors for the church, the body of Christ. In reality, the church is me and you. Let's talk about what that means to us as a family.

- What's your favorite part about going to church?
- How many people do you think it takes to have a church service?
- What do you think God likes the most about His children going to church? The music, Communion, the giving, the sermon, or the fellowship? Or do you think He likes all of it equally?
- Is it still a church if a group of tribal people meet together under a tree to talk about God, sing songs to Him, and pray? Why or why not?

Remember, the church isn't a building; it's God's people. Some churches meet in big buildings and some in small buildings. Some gather in rented schools or shopping malls or even theaters. In fact, some churches meet in homes. That's how the church began shortly after Jesus' time on Earth. The earliest churches met in people's homes. The important thing is that God's people gather to worship Him and grow together as a community.

CHURCH

Scripture Reading: Hebrews 10:24–25

When the apostle Peter described the church, he compared it to stones that are brought together for a greater purpose. He said, "[Just as you come to Christ], a living stone—rejected by men but chosen and valuable to God—you yourselves, as living stones, are being built into a spiritual house for a holy priesthood to offer spiritual sacrifices acceptable to God through Jesus Christ" (1 Peter 2:4–5).

Peter described the church as a "spiritual house" made up of people. People are the church. In the book of Ephesians, the apostle Paul wrote,

> You are no longer foreigners and strangers, but fellow citizens with the saints, and members of God's household, built on the foundation of the apostles and prophets, with Christ Jesus Himself as the cornerstone. The whole building, being put together by Him, grows into a holy sanctuary in the Lord. You also are being built together for God's dwelling in the Spirit.   Ephesians 2:19–22

In this passage, the people in the church are referred to as a "whole building" and a "sanctuary." Our purpose is to be a place where God's Spirit can dwell among us as a group.

Let's take a moment to reenact a church service right now. It's a great way to remind us that church isn't about "where" worship happens. What matters is that God's people join together to fulfill His purposes.

We can close in prayer and thank God for His people, the church, who are the hands and heart of Jesus in a hurting world.

CHURCH

SCRIPTURE READING: MATTHEW 16:18

Every Sunday during football season, National Football League (NFL) stadiums are packed across the United States. Fans gather to celebrate their favorite teams. They fight traffic, dress in team colors, and spend most of the day preparing for the game.

During the game they scream and shout and cheer on their teams. When the game's over and they finally get home, they turn on SportsCenter to watch the replays. After all is said and done, these devoted football fans spend about seven hours on the whole experience. Though the fans and the players don't know one another, the fans still think it's worthwhile giving the game and the players their entire day.

If the NFL can get hundreds of thousands of fans to cheer on players they don't even know, why is the church not packed every Sunday with even more excitement to celebrate the Giver of Life?

Name some places where people go to enthusiastically cheer on their teams for hours at a time. *(Encourage responses.)* Why do you think these people are willing to spend their time and energy like that?

What would happen if Christians gave God the same level of enthusiasm they give to entertainment and sports? Would that change the atmosphere of our church on Sunday or other days of the week? Why is God deserving of our worship, praise, and enthusiasm?

Let's pray together right now and thank God for who He is and what He means to us.

CHURCH

SCRIPTURE READING: 1 CORINTHIANS 3:17

Today for Fun Friday we're going to play the Chatter Bee game. This is how it's played: Two family members will stand back to back. At a signal, they'll both turn around, face each other, and talk nonstop for thirty seconds. Both must talk about what the church is and what we learned about the church this week.

Another family member will watch the two and time them. At the end of thirty seconds, this person will decide who was the best talker. The criteria for choosing the winner is whoever spoke most clearly on the topic, hesitated the least, was the most creative, and gave the best information.

For the next activity, we'll find out what it's like to preach a sermon. Each family member will prepare a minisermon and will have three minutes to deliver it. The sermon must be about the church, and you're free to preach from the Bible verses we used on previous days this week. The rest of us will sit and listen and take notes just as .we'd normally do at church.

(Each person gets a turn preaching. After everyone has delivered their sermons, close the "church service" with a word of prayer.)

FEAR

SCRIPTURE READING: ISAIAH 41:10

Fear is a powerful emotion. It can have a good purpose in our lives, such as keeping us from doing harmful things. For example, putting your hand on a hot stove wouldn't be wise. For most people—even very young children—the fear of burning their hands will prevent them from touching a hot stove.

Fear can also motivate you to complete your homework when you may not want to. It could be the fear of getting a bad grade or a zero on the assignment. Fear isn't always bad.

In the Bible, God frequently tells us to fear Him. He doesn't mean He wants us to fear Him in the same way we would fear a monster in a scary show. When we read that we're to fear God, it means that we're to take Him seriously. We're to show Him the reverence and awe He deserves. Reverence simply means that we show Him great respect and honor.

Fear can also be a bad thing. When you're afraid of a storm, a show, a person, a sickness, or even the future, God wants to calm your fears. He wants you to put your trust in Him whenever you're afraid.

Talk about a time you were afraid. It might have been during a storm with lightning or thunder, or even at school when you had to give a speech. Did you pray and ask God to calm your fears? If you did, what happened?

What is one way you can remind yourself to pray when you're afraid?

Let's come up with some creative ways to remind ourselves to trust God whenever we're afraid.

We'll close in prayer, thanking God for His presence in our lives, even when we are afraid.

FEAR

SCRIPTURE READING: 2 TIMOTHY 1:7

When Peter was with the disciples on a boat in the middle of the Sea of Galilee, they were caught in a big storm. They were afraid, but Jesus came walking to them on top of the water. When Peter saw Jesus walking on the water, he asked if he could join him, and Jesus told him to come. But when Peter began walking on the water, the wind and the waves distracted him. He took his eyes off Jesus, and the terrible storm filled him with fear.

Because he looked away from Jesus, Peter began to sink beneath the waves. But Jesus rescued him. He "immediately . . . reached out His hand, caught hold of [Peter], and said to him, 'You of little faith, why did you doubt?'" (Matthew 14:31). Peter's fear led to doubt. Fear has a way of doing that. But Jesus asks us to put our faith in Him and not be afraid.

Let's act out this story in the Bible right now. One person will be Peter climbing out of the boat and walking toward Jesus on the water. Another person will be Jesus walking on the water. The rest of us will be the wind and waves or the other disciples in the boat.

We can take turns playing different roles, but the main idea is to act out what happened. We want to truly understand how Jesus rescued Peter when Peter turned his fears over to the Lord.

FEAR

SCRIPTURE READING: 1 JOHN 4:18

All of us are afraid at one time or other. Some of us are afraid of the dark. Others are afraid of dogs. Some are afraid of scary movies. You don't need to be embarrassed about being afraid. But God does want to help you overcome your fears. One thing that helps is to change how you view whatever makes you afraid.

When a parent or another trusted adult lifts up a little child, that child suddenly has a different way of looking at things. He or she can see the world from a higher perspective. Like a parent picking up a child, God wants us to feel safe in His arms.

Let's read more about gaining this new perspective and finding courage in His Word.

> *Be strong and courageous; don't be terrified or afraid of [your enemies]. For it is the LORD your God who goes with you; He will not leave you or forsake you.* DEUTERONOMY 31:6

> *I sought the LORD, and He answered me and delivered me from all my fears.* PSALM 34:4

> *When I am afraid, I will trust in You.* PSALM 56:3

> *Do not fear, for I am with you; do not be afraid, for I am your God. I will strengthen you; I will help you; I will hold on to you with My righteous right hand.* ISAIAH 41:10

Choose one of these verses and turn it into a song right now. Add a little melody to it and maybe some extra words. You can work on your song alone if you prefer. Or we can work in teams of two or together as a family to create one song, with each of us adding words and ideas.

Nonmusical families may choose to instead create decorative posters using one of the verses with artwork. Or share a scary experience and discuss how a particular verse helped or could help. Did the verse change your perspective on the situation? Did it calm your fears and make you feel safe? Did you feel Jesus' presence in the midst of fear?

FEAR

SCRIPTURE READING: PSALM 34:4

Even though the journey of life is exciting, a variety of things in this world can make us fearful. Some scary situations can seem like a big gorilla running right at you. Have you ever been to the zoo? Talk about how you felt when you saw a big animal like a gorilla or a tiger. Were you afraid? Why or why not?

You might not have been afraid because you knew that the glass or the cage would protect you. But all sorts of things in life can make you afraid, whether it's a difficult exam at school, saying no when a friend wants you to do something wrong, needing to apologize to someone you may have hurt, or meeting a distant relative for the first time.

These situations might make you want to run away and hide instead of facing up to them. It's not unusual for people to avoid scary situations. But running away doesn't stop them from happening. If you run to your heavenly Father and let Him wrap His arms around you, it will change your fear of facing scary situations. God's love and care can give you strength and courage.

Name one kind of scary situation when you could run to the Lord.

Can you think of a Bible story where a person, or a group of people, had every reason to be afraid but decided to trust in the Lord instead? *(Be prepared to give an example.)* What was the result?

FEAR

SCRIPTURE READING: PHILIPPIANS 4:6

Fear isn't fun. But for today's Fun Friday activity, we're going to play a game of hopscotch. If you've never played hopscotch before, here's how to do it:

1. Draw ten large squares with chalk on the driveway, the patio, or some surface that's made of concrete. Draw the first three squares one on top of the other. Then draw the next two squares side by side, followed by two squares, one after the other. Draw two more squares side by side and then one more square after those two.

2. Next, number each square. The first square is number one, and so on.

3. Get a small rock and write the word *fear* on it.

4. Each player will take a turn throwing the rock of fear onto a numbered square. You can't step on the square where the fear rock lands. You'll hop on all the other squares up and back on just one foot, but you'll have to jump over the square with the fear rock.

5. Take turns until each player has successfully gone through the hopscotch course, hopping on all nine squares, one by one, on one foot, while avoiding the square with the fear rock.

This game illustrates how we can get past our fears. Sometimes we have to push through our fears to get to the other side of a challenge or circumstance. Remember this principle: When you're afraid, put your trust in God. He is there with you, and He'll help calm your fears. Keep your eyes on Jesus and not on whatever is causing you to be afraid.

DISCIPLESHIP

SCRIPTURE READING: MATTHEW 28:18–20

The planet Mercury is hot. Pluto is no longer called a planet, but it's still very cold. Why is one planet cold and the other hot? Mercury is really close to the sun, and Pluto is a long way off.

The farther a planet is from our sun, the colder things become. But the closer a planet is, the hotter things are. You may not be a Pluto Christian or a Mercury Christian. Maybe you're an Earth Christian who is both hot and cold. You may be a seasonal Christian who changes depending on whether it's winter, summer, spring, or fall.

God is looking for some Mercury Christians, people who are hot all the time because they stay close to His *Son*.

When we're close to God, we naturally live as His disciples. Being a disciple means that you follow someone, doing what your leader says and following what he or she teaches. If you're a disciple of Jesus, you'll do what He says in His Word. Your life will also show the fruit of the Spirit: "love, joy, peace, patience, kindness, goodness, faith, gentleness, [and] self-control" (Galatians 5:22–23). That's the distinguishing mark of a Christ follower. Though none of us follows Jesus perfectly, if we're seeking to trust and obey Him each day, He'll grow His fruit in our lives.

God wants you to be His disciple. He wants you to learn His Word and His desires for your life so you'll reflect Him to others.

Let's each draw a picture of a fruit tree. On it we'll list the different fruits of the Spirit described in Galatians 5:22–23. Make each fruit a different color so it stands apart. If you need help writing the words for each fruit, ask for help.

DISCIPLESHIP

SCRIPTURE READING: MATTHEW 5:14–16

This week we're learning about the importance of discipleship. A disciple is one who believes in Jesus Christ and visibly follows His example. It's one thing to believe in Jesus, but it's another thing to follow His example in the way we live our lives.

As disciples, we're also teaching others about Jesus Christ so they might believe and follow His example. It's as if we're duplicating the image of Christ, because excellent disciples are seeking to be Jesus look-alikes.

Let's talk about this in more detail. What is discipleship? What does it mean to live by following the example Jesus set? How can we teach others to do the same?

Think of it like a family with parents and children. What things do children do just like their parents? What do you do just like us? *(As parents, you can share the ways you're like your mom and dad, and your kids can express how they think they're like you, whether in mannerisms or conduct.)* How did you become like us?

Discipleship means that Jesus Christ is your parent, and as His child, you take on His mannerisms and conduct.

DISCIPLESHIP

SCRIPTURE READING: LUKE 14:27

As disciples of Jesus, we should look like Him. When people see us, they should recognize Jesus in us—His love, grace, power, faith, and more. For His essence (His character) to be fully visible in our lives, we must actively pursue Him as our teacher and leader.

Let's look at what God's Word says about discipleship.

A disciple is not above his teacher, but everyone who is fully trained will be like his teacher. LUKE 6:40

Jesus said to the Jews who had believed Him, "If you continue in My word, you really are My disciples. You will know the truth, and the truth will set you free." JOHN 8:31–32

I give you a new command: Love one another. Just as I have loved you, you must also love one another. By this all people will know that you are My disciples, if you have love for one another. JOHN 13:34–35

God tells us that we'll be like Jesus when we are His disciples. We'll love one another and reflect His love for others through our lives. One way we do this is by reading and studying God's Word.

Name five other practical ways we can show God's love to the people in our lives. Let's each make an effort to do all five this week.

DISCIPLESHIP

SCRIPTURE READING: 2 TIMOTHY 2:2

Coach Thomas was in charge of the junior basketball team at his church. He taught the kids to focus and play together as a team. He always gave his kids the solid coaching they needed to be the best basketball players they could be. Coach Thomas was a great basketball player himself, starting in juniors when he was young and playing all the way through college. All he did with his church team was take the lessons he learned as a player and pass them on to the kids he was now coaching.

The story of Coach Thomas is the story of discipleship. He spent a lot of his time helping others become their best. He took his experiences and knowledge and did his best to teach his players to be just as successful as he was.

In the same way, Jesus Christ wants you to be His disciple. He wants you to learn the Bible so that you'll understand exactly how to live with excellence. He has been through all the experiences of life that qualify Him as the best coach ever. Your job is to learn from Jesus and follow Him as the head coach of the Christian team, and then put yourself in a position where you can coach others.

As a family, let's make a list of ten qualities we believe Jesus would want us to have as His disciples. They could be qualities like patience, a joyful heart, and a respectful mind. We can come up with any number of ideas, but they should all be qualities we believe Jesus wants us to have. When we've finished our list, let's talk about each quality.

After our discussion, we'll close in prayer and ask God to guide us to be His disciples in every way possible.

DISCIPLESHIP

SCRIPTURE READING: LUKE 9:23

Did you know that when you buy a CD or download a song, you aren't getting the original recording? You're getting what's called a *replica*. The original recording is called the *master*. The replicas of the master sound just like the master, but they aren't the master.

Jesus is the master, and He wants to copy Himself onto His followers. That way, when people see you or me, they see a replica of the Master. As disciples, our role is to follow the Master, who has all authority.

As you get to know Jesus and abide in Him, He will be more and more visible in your life. To abide with Jesus means staying connected with Him, like branches are connected to a vine. How does that work? Whenever you think of Him and trust him, you're with Him. Whenever you read your Bible, choose to trust and obey Him, pray, listen to praise music, and worship Him, you're abiding in Him.

Jesus wants to be in your life more often than once a week at church. He wants to be a regular part of your thoughts and actions as you grow as His disciple.

For our Fun Friday activity, we're going to make some juice or lemonade. First, we'll start by pouring water into a pitcher. Then we'll follow the instructions on the packet or the can of frozen juice concentrate.

What happens to the water when we pour the contents of the packet or the sugar into it? It changes, doesn't it? It may even change colors.

This is a great illustration of what it means to abide in Jesus. Abiding in Him means living so close to Jesus that He literally changes us into His likeness, and we take on His qualities and characteristics throughout our lives.

Let's pray and ask God to help us learn to abide in Christ and become more like Him every day.

OBEDIENCE

SCRIPTURE READING: JOHN 14:15

What is obedience? It simply means to do with the right spirit what someone has asked us to do. It's easy to obey someone who tells us to do something we like to do. For example, if you're hungry for fried chicken, and your stomach tells you to get some, you don't mind obeying. But if one of us tells you to drink a spinach smoothie, that's another story. You might not be so excited about obeying then!

When we or your teachers ask you to do something you don't mind doing, you probably do it easily. You may even have a smile on your face. But what about those times when we ask you to take out the trash, clean the kitchen, or finish your math homework? It's not as easy, is it?

There's a difference between obeying just for the sake of obeying and obeying with the right spirit. Have you ever obeyed but had a wrong attitude? How did it show? Did you pout or put off doing the task for a long time? Maybe you did a sloppy job. Whatever the case, a right heart matters greatly when it comes to obeying God the way He wants us to.

One way to obey with a right spirit is to remember that obeying a person in authority is the same as obeying God (as long as that person isn't demanding that you do something you know is wrong). God is happy with your obedience, so think of Him smiling whenever you obey. And if you ever feel yucky about whatever you have to do, ask Him to give you the right spirit so you'll do the task in a way He would be proud of.

OBEDIENCE

SCRIPTURE READING: ACTS 5:29

This week we're learning about the importance of obedience. Obeying simply means to do what you're told and, more specifically, to do what God says.

Obedience is not only essential because it shows that you can follow directions; it's extremely important because it lets God know that you love Him. Jesus said, "If you love Me, you will keep My commands" (John 14:15). It's one thing to say that you love God, but it's another to demonstrate your love by obeying Him.

Let's talk about how we show our love to God through obedience. In what ways have you been obedient to God this week? How could you have been more obedient? How important is obedience now that you know it's connected to your love for God? How can you do better next week at obeying us and, most of all, God?

Let's pray together and ask God to help us demonstrate our love for Him through our obedience.

OBEDIENCE

SCRIPTURE READING: 1 PETER 1:14

G od is looking out for our best interests when He asks us to live obediently.

Let's look at the kind of heart God wants each of us to have when we obey. Another term for "obey" in the Scriptures is *submit*. The apostle Peter talked about household servants, who were called slaves, submitting to their masters, but the principle of obedience and submission applies to all of us. Here's what Peter said:

> *Household slaves, submit with all fear to your masters, not only to the good and gentle but also to the cruel. For it brings favor if, mindful of God's will, someone endures grief from suffering unjustly. For what credit is there if you sin and are punished, and you endure it? But when you do what is good and suffer, if you endure it, this brings favor with God.*
>
> *For you were called to this, because Christ also suffered for you, leaving you an example, so that you should follow in His steps.*
>
> 1 PETER 2:18–21

What we learn from this passage is that even if we don't like what we're being asked to do—as long as it isn't wrong—if we obey with a right heart, it will bring us favor with God. Even if no one else sees, God will see, and He knows our hearts. He'll reward us with His favor (which means His goodness and blessings) when we willingly and joyfully submit to Him and obey.

OBEDIENCE

SCRIPTURE READING: 1 JOHN 5:3

Have you ever played Simon Says? In this game, you do only what Simon says. If Simon says, "Raise your arms," you must raise your arms. If Simon says, "Jump in the air," you must jump in the air. But you obey *only* when the person giving the instructions includes the words "Simon says" before telling you to do something.

If you obey the instructions when the person hasn't said "Simon says," you're out of the game. The key to Simon Says is making sure you're obedient only to Simon.

Most kids lose the game because they get distracted when other players make mistakes. If you watch the others around you, you begin to focus on the wrong instructions. To win you must focus only on the leader—Simon. Once you start copying what everyone else is doing, you're no longer focusing on what Simon is saying. If you follow the actions of someone who isn't listening, you'll get kicked out of the game with that person.

As Christians we need to play a new game called God Says. The key to winning in the Christian life is obeying only what God says and not focusing on what everyone else is doing.

Let's play Simon Says right now. While we do, remember how important it is to listen to the person in charge and not be misled by what other people do.

OBEDIENCE

SCRIPTURE READING: PSALM 119:30

O bedience requires listening to directions and understanding the leader's expectations. Then we have to fulfill those expectations. For today's Fun Friday activity, let's play a little game that will help us practice listening and obeying. You may have played it before. It's called Red Light, Green Light. Here are the rules:

1. Designate a starting line and a finish line with as much room in between the lines as the space will allow, preferably twenty feet.
2. One of the players is the stoplight. This person stands at the finish line.
3. Everyone else lines up at the starting line.
4. The stoplight player begins by either saying "red light" or "green light." When the other players hear the words *green light*, they walk as fast as they can toward the finish line.
5. Players must stop whenever they hear the words *red light*.
6. Any player who doesn't stop immediately at the words *red light* must immediately return to the starting line.
7. The stoplight player continues to call out commands until one player reaches the finish line. This is the winner.

(After playing the game, discuss some of the lessons everyone learned about the importance of listening and obeying.)

What did you learn from the game about listening and obeying? What makes obeying easier and what doesn't? Share a time when you didn't want to obey but managed to do it with the right spirit. Why do you think you were able to do that?

GREATNESS

SCRIPTURE READING: JOB 37:5

Greatness is a standard. It involves doing everything with excellence. It isn't perfection, but it's achieving and performing at your highest level. One person's greatness may be different from another's. One person might have athletic gifts; another might be brilliant at math. Greatness shouldn't be measured by comparing yourself to someone else. It should be measured by comparing yourself to the standard of excellence that the Lord has for you (which is not God's perfect standard that only Jesus reached).

Have you ever seen somebody dunk a basketball? What would you think if the person lowered the basket before dunking the ball? Would you be impressed? Probably not. The reason it's fun to see a basketball dunked is because it's such a difficult challenge. Lowering the standard takes away the greatness.

God has a standard. He has a goal. Greatness is that goal. Yet too many people lower His standard and then congratulate themselves for being able to "dunk the ball."

Let's keep His standard where it needs to be. Little by little, as we continue to put in the effort, we'll reach that goal. To illustrate today's lesson, let's shoot some hoops!

(If you have a basketball hoop, take turns shooting the ball to see how many baskets each family member can make. If you don't have a hoop, you can use a regular basket—such as a laundry basket—and play Toss the Socks. See how many family members can toss a knotted sock into the basket, standing as far away as they choose.)

GREATNESS

SCRIPTURE READING: LUKE 1:15

This week we're talking about true greatness. Who doesn't want to be great in one way or another? It's okay to desire greatness. The problem lies in pursing greatness in the wrong way. In our culture, many people try to achieve greatness through popularity, wealth, or fame.

In reality, greatness isn't based on what we do or what we have. It has to do with who we are. It depends on growing into the person God wants each of us to be. If you're popular in the world but aren't in a consistently growing relationship with God, then you aren't great.

Jesus is great because He did the will of His Father and helped many people. True greatness is found only in being like Jesus, who is the greatest person of all.

In what ways can you become great like Jesus? What do you think God wants you to do to with your life? If you listen to God and obey Him like Jesus did, you'll find your greatness.

GREATNESS

SCRIPTURE READING: PSALM 71:21

Greatness is maximizing our potential for the glory of God and the good of others.

The apostle Paul urged those in the church at Thessalonica to "excel still more" in obeying God's commands (1 Thessalonians 4:1, NASB). He urged the Corinthian believers to "always [abound] in the work of the Lord" (1 Corinthians 15:58, NASB) and to seek greatness in all they did.

To want to be great is a good thing. God wants us to be great. Jesus said so. In John 14:12, He told His disciples, "Truly, truly, I say to you, he who believes in Me, the works that I do, he will do also; and greater works than these he will do" (NASB). Jesus said plainly that if we believe in Him, and walk in the Spirit, we're going to do things that even He didn't get to do on Earth. That's a powerful reality none of us should miss. That is a kingdom truth. Not only will we do the great things Jesus did, but we'll also do even greater things.

Jesus never traveled more than a few hundred miles from the place of His birth during His earthly ministry. Yet Christ followers who have spread the gospel around the world have gone on to do even greater works than Jesus. If Jesus said that we'll do "greater works" than He did, God evidently doesn't have a problem with greatness.

Let's make a list of some of the things Jesus did that made Him great. How are people doing great things in His name today?

Share what you dream of doing one day for the Lord. Then we'll close in prayer, asking God to prepare each of us to serve Him with greatness.

GREATNESS

SCRIPTURE READING: LAMENTATIONS 3:23

When a company develops a marketing campaign around their product, they come up with ideas to make their product's greatness stand out from the competition. Two of these key components are the logo and the tagline.

Let's draw our own personal logos. Make sure yours reflects who you are as a person—strong, quiet, solid, dreamy, and so on. Choose qualities that God holds up as great. Some examples are humility, kindness, and love. Think about how you can stand out in the world as a reflection of Jesus.

After drawing your logo, develop a tagline that lets others know who you are in a simple yet creative statement.

Here are some sample taglines:

Nike: "Just do it"
Apple: "Think different"
McDonald's: "I'm lovin' it"
Milk: "Got milk?"
M&M's: "Melts in your mouth, not in your hands"
The Urban Alternative: "Teaching truth, transforming lives"

Let's share our personal taglines and talk about why we chose them.

We can close in prayer, thanking God for making us each unique and calling us to live our lives for Him.

GREATNESS

SCRIPTURE READING: PSALM 145:3

Have you ever been jealous of a sister or brother or other family member? Or how about someone in school? Maybe that person got more attention than you. That might be similar to what happened with two of Jesus' disciples. They provide an example of how to pursue greatness Jesus' way.

When James and John, known as the Sons of Thunder, sought a place of honor in Christ's kingdom, the other ten disciples got jealous. They gave the brothers a hard time for expressing their desire for greatness.

However, Jesus never corrected the two men for wanting to be great. After all, He knew how they were formed. He knew what was inside them. He knew that their desire for greatness in the kingdom of God wasn't wrong. Jesus only corrected how they wanted to accomplish their goal. He said, "You know that the rulers of the Gentiles lord it over them, and their great men exercise authority over them. It is not this way among you, but whoever wishes to become great among you shall be your servant" (Matthew 20:25–26, NASB).

Jesus didn't tell the brothers not to wish to be great. He told them not to achieve greatness or use it the same way the Gentiles did.

True greatness is outward focused and others driven.

For our Fun Friday activity, each of us will get to create a word-art collage. Draw the word *great* in big bubble letters on a piece of paper or poster board. Then draw pictures inside the letters. The pictures should illustrate acts of true greatness.

UNITY

Scripture Reading: Philippians 2:2

Christian unity begins with the relational oneness we share with one another because of God's work in our lives through the Holy Spirit. We're closest to unity when we allow the Spirit to do His work in us, and when we point to and celebrate that work.

Where do you see the Spirit most at work in our family?

How are you pointing to and celebrating the Spirit's work in our home and in our family? Can you name one example of a time you and other family members showed unity in working toward a common goal?

How does unity help our home be more peaceful and productive?

A great illustration of unity involves mayonnaise. When making mayonnaise, it's difficult to get the oil and the water to come together. Oil and water don't mix, but they're necessary ingredients in mayonnaise.

So the makers of mayonnaise introduced an emulsifier in the ingredients. An emulsifier helps ingredients that are at odds with each other to get along. So a necessary ingredient in mayonnaise is the emulsifier: eggs.

The eggs say, "I want you, oil, to hang out with me, and I want you, water, to hang out with me too." When eggs get mixed in with the water and the oil, those ingredients will now hang out with each other. Not because water and oil like each other but because both of them can agree on liking the eggs. As a result, something greater than the individual parts is created from this new unity. We call it mayonnaise.

Let's close in prayer, asking God to help us learn to walk together in unity.

UNITY

SCRIPTURE READING: 1 PETER 3:8

This week we're learning about the importance of unity. Unity doesn't mean trying to be the same as others around you. It means that you and others are going in the same direction with a single purpose or goal.

Your efforts are multiplied when you join with other people in unity. That's why Jesus prayed for unity among the people of God. Here's what He prayed:

I do not ask on behalf of these alone, but for those also who believe in Me through their word; that they may all be one; even as You, Father, are in Me and I in You, that they also may be in Us, so that the world may believe that You sent Me.

The glory which You have given Me I have given to them, that they may be one, just as We are one; I in them and You in Me, that they may be perfected in unity, so that the world may know that You sent Me, and loved them, even as You have loved Me.
JOHN 17:20–23, NASB

Jesus knew that if the people of God come together as one unit, they'd be able to accomplish great things.

Your hand can't do much if only the pinky finger is doing the work, but if all the fingers join in, it has the ability to do many powerful things. We see this truth very clearly in the world of sports.

Which sports require a team to be unified to win? How can playing sports help us learn the concept of unity?

How can you be a better team player in our family for the purpose of unity?

Let's pray right now and ask God to help us work together to be the family He wants us to be.

UNITY

SCRIPTURE READING: 1 CORINTHIANS 1:10

For today's Wednesday in the Word, we're going to look up a Bible passage. Open your Bible and turn to Ephesians 4. Every time you see the word *one* or a word that means "one," underline or highlight it.

How many times did you find those words? *(Give time for answers.)* That's a lot. Do you think someone was trying to make a point? What point do you think the apostle Paul (the writer of Ephesians) was trying to make?

Remember, unity isn't uniformity or sameness. It isn't about everybody being like everybody else. God created things in different shapes, colors, sizes, and styles. Yet everything He created, according to Psalm 19, was set in place for the sole purpose of testifying to the "glory of God" (verse 1).

In sports, unity doesn't mean that every player on the field or in the stadium plays the same position. Each athlete is unique in his or her talents, skills, identity, and responsibilities, but everyone on the team is headed for the same goal line. If it's a basketball team, the five players on the court may play different positions, but the goal they're shooting at is the same.

Try to imagine everyone playing the same position on a soccer team or a basketball team. What if everyone on a soccer team was a goalie? What would happen in a game? Not much, actually. Keep that in mind when you think about unity. It doesn't mean you're to be just like everyone else. People are made up of different races and personalities and even nationalities. But it does mean working together on the same game plan for the same goal. That's unity.

UNITY

Scripture Reading: Colossians 3:14

What if we were all alike? What if everyone was the same color and the same height and wore the same clothes? It would be hard to tell each of us apart, wouldn't it? Remember, unity isn't uniformity, so it doesn't mean we all act alike. It simply means that we all work toward the same goal. As Christians, our goal is to glorify God and make Him known to those around us.

Let's each draw a picture or cut pictures out of magazines to make a collage illustrating unity. Be sure to draw or choose images of people who are very different, because we want to emphasize that unity doesn't mean we're all the same. It means we have the same goal.

After we've finished our collages, let's each think of a goal that the people in our pictures might be working toward. We'll go around the room and share the goals we thought of; then we'll discuss ways these people might need to work together to accomplish the goals.

In what ways can you have more unity with our family or with your classmates at school? List two things you can do this week to help bring about a more unified atmosphere around your life and your choices.

God loves it when we work together for good. It brings Him glory.

Let's close in prayer and ask God to help us live in unity in ways that reflect His character and love.

UNITY

SCRIPTURE READING: 2 CORINTHIANS 13:11

For today's Fun Friday activity, we're going to play the Straw and Pea Relay to remind us how important it is to work together in unity. *(Gather some bowls, dried peas, and straws in preparation for this activity.)* Each person gets his or her own straw.

To start, we'll divide our family into small teams. *(If you can, make sure there's an even number of people on each team.)* Each team gets two bowls. Put one bowl on one side of the room and fill it with fifteen dried peas. Then place an empty bowl on the other side of the room.

Each player has to suck up a pea with the end of the straw and transfer it all the way over to the empty bowl. If the pea falls, the player has to go back and start again. The first team to get all its peas across the room and into the other bowl wins. *(Keep an eye on younger children so they don't accidentally inhale a pea.)*

This relay is a fun way to learn that unity is important, because a team has no chance of winning if only one player works toward the goal of filling the bowl but the others don't join in.

Let's be sure to cheer on our teammates while they're playing, because unity also means encouraging one another as we work toward the same goal!

ETERNITY

SCRIPTURE READING: PSALM 90:2

*E*ternity. *Heaven.* Those are big words we don't always know how to explain. Take a moment and share what you think heaven and eternity will be like. *(Encourage everyone to share their thoughts.)*

The more you talk about heaven, the more you may wish you could experience some of heaven right now. It seems like a really awesome place, doesn't it?

Well, you can experience heaven in one way. God has given us the Holy Spirit as the "pledge" or down payment on our redemption (Ephesians 1:13–14). The Spirit's presence in our lives is God's assurance that someday He'll complete our salvation by taking us to heaven.

In the meantime, it's the Holy Spirit's job to give us a taste of heaven today. The Holy Spirit wants to lift our spirits so we can have a heavenly experience even while we're on Earth.

Our anticipation of heaven is like the story of Cinderella. Cinderella had to live with a wicked stepmother and two wicked stepsisters, but when she went to the ball, she met a prince. And even though she had to go back to her hard life for a while, she was never the same, because her prince didn't forget her. One day he came and took her away to his castle to be his bride.

Right now you and I have to live with a wicked stepmother called the Devil and wicked stepsisters called demons. This world is also filled with sin, and sometimes our lives can be hard because we're living under sin's curse.

But God wants us to remember that even while we're ironing clothes and scrubbing floors, the prince named Jesus Christ is coming back to get us someday and take us to be with Him forever.

That's heaven, and it's going to be awesome!

Let's pray together and thank God for His gift of heaven and His promise of hope.

ETERNITY

SCRIPTURE READING: ECCLESIASTES 3:11

This week we're learning about the concept of eternity. Eternity has no beginning and no end.

God is an eternal being. Think about it: There has never been a time when God has not existed. God wasn't created, so He had no starting point. You have a birthday, but God doesn't. We celebrate the birth of Jesus Christ on Christmas, but Jesus lived before He was born on this earth. Even when Jesus died on the cross, rose from the dead, and ascended to heaven, He continued to be eternal.

When we go to heaven to be with God, we will be entering eternity. This means we'll enter a new life with no end because we'll be with God. How much fun do you think it would be to always be able to play, sing, dance, and enjoy yourself with God without having to stop?

This simple illustration can give us a better understanding of eternity. Imagine the Pacific Ocean being emptied of all its water. Then every million years, a bird drops one grain of sand into the empty space. How long might it take the bird to fill the space with sand? (It's obviously an unfathomable amount of time.) Well, whenever that bird finally finishes its task, you will have been in eternity with God only ten minutes. Eternity is timeless.

Let's pray, asking God to help us grasp these big ideas and live in the light of His love and eternal grace.

ETERNITY

SCRIPTURE READING: JOHN 17:3

There's no better place to learn about this mysterious subject of eternity than in the Bible. Let's see what God's Word says about it.

Before the mountains were born, before You gave birth to the earth and the world, from eternity to eternity, You are God. PSALM 90:2

How long is "eternity to eternity"?

I [Jesus] assure you: Anyone who hears My word and believes Him who sent Me has eternal life and will not come under judgment but has passed from death to life. JOHN 5:24

How do we know that we have eternal life?

[God] has made everything appropriate in its time. He has also put eternity in their hearts, but man cannot discover the work God has done from beginning to end. ECCLESIASTES 3:11

What do you think it means that God has "put eternity" in our hearts?

God loved the world in this way: He gave His One and Only Son, so that everyone who believes in Him will not perish but have eternal life. JOHN 3:16

Let's say this verse over and over until we can say it by heart.

Eternity is going to be a really long time. In fact, there will be no end to eternity. When we compare our time, days, and life on Earth to what we'll experience in eternity, our lives here will be just a dot on a time line, like a speck we can barely see.

It's good to live with that mind-set because it will impact our decisions for good. Thinking about eternity encourages us to seek God and His will, because what we do for Him is the only thing that will last forever.

ETERNITY

SCRIPTURE READING: JOHN 5:24

We live in a world where time is everything, so everything we do must be done within a certain time. For example, you have to wake up at a certain time to get ready for the day. You have to get to school at a certain time so you won't be penalized for being late. Even birthdays, anniversaries, and holidays happen at the same time every year. That helps people measure how far they've come or how old they are.

In fact, time is so important to people that many say they'd ask for more of it if they were granted just one wish.

Would you like to have more time in the day? If you did, what kinds of things would you want to do with the extra time?

Everything in the human world begins, ends, and happens based on time. But time doesn't limit God the way it limits us. God isn't bound by time; rather, He exists outside of time. He doesn't even need to wear a watch!

God isn't crunched for time to try to make things happen, but things happen whenever He says it's time. Eternity is God's home and God's nature.

Let's count together to sixty at a pace that's about a second for each number. As we do, think about the fact that in heaven there will be no time. Those sixty seconds you just counted will seem less than the blink of an eye. That's why the apostle Peter said that "with the Lord one day is like a thousand years, and a thousand years like one day" (2 Peter 3:8). We won't even think about seconds, hours, days, or years!

Let's read Psalm 90:4 aloud and then share our thoughts about what that verse means in our everyday lives.

ETERNITY

SCRIPTURE READING: REVELATION 22:5

Here on Earth, it's impossible for us to see God clearly or know Him fully. The fog in our minds gets in the way. But one day in heaven, the fog will disappear, and we'll see God as He really is.

The apostle Paul described it like this: "Now we see in a mirror dimly, but then face to face; now I know in part, but then I will know fully just as I also have been fully known" (1 Corinthians 13:12, NASB).

(To illustrate this passage, find a mirror. It could be a pocket mirror or a handheld mirror. Then boil some water on the stove. Add enough water to the pot so that when it boils, there will be lots of steam. Caution: Keep all children away from the boiling water.

When the water boils, place the mirror over the water in such a way that the steam will fog the glass.

An alternate illustration is to let the shower run on hot until steam appears. Then put the mirror in the steam.)

For our Fun Friday activity, let's try a little experiment. First, I'll boil some water and hold a mirror over it for a few seconds. Then I'll pass the mirror around the room. Look in the mirror while the glass is fogged over. What do you see? Describe how hard it is to recognize details, especially faraway details.

After everyone has looked in the mirror, I'll wipe it off with a rag or towel so that it's clean. Now look again. Can you see things clearly now?

That's what Paul meant when he said that "we see in a mirror dimly." Right now we don't understand very many eternal things at all. But when we reach eternity, we'll understand everything clearly, including God, angels, and even ourselves.

Our knowledge will be perfect in heaven because we'll see God face-to-face (Revelation 22:4). In other words, nothing will cloud our vision or keep us from seeing God as He really is.

WISDOM

SCRIPTURE READING: JAMES 1:5

L ife is full of decisions. Like many people, you might just be tired of making the wrong ones. Have you ever made a bad choice? Some of us are still feeling the effects of the bad choices we've made in the past.

If you were given special coins to exchange for a chance to leap backward in time and redo something, would you take them? What choices might you have made differently in the past? Would you make better choices knowing what you know now?

Or how about your time? Would you pick different ways of spending it? Would you have practiced harder at whatever sport, gift, or skill you have? Would you have studied more?

If you answered yes to any of these questions, then you know what it means to apply wisdom to life's situations. Because that's exactly what you want to do. By answering yes, you want to go back and make a different choice, this time with the wisdom of hindsight.

Wisdom is the ability to not only understand the best way to approach something or someone but also to do it. Wisdom might be a noun in English class, but when it comes to living your life, it's a verb—an action.

But wisdom doesn't do you a bit of good stuck in your brain. You access the power of wisdom to succeed in life only by applying it.

Let's pray together now and ask God to grant us His wisdom each day as we make choices.

WISDOM

SCRIPTURE READING: PROVERBS 3:13–18

This week we're learning about an important topic called wisdom. Wisdom involves our ability to take in information and use it correctly. To be wise doesn't mean we just have knowledge. It means we use that knowledge the right way. A person can be very smart but not have wisdom. In other words, some people go to church and listen to the Word of God, but they never become wise. They hear the Word of God but are unable to put it into practice in their lives.

The question is not "What do you know?" The question is "What will you do with what you know?"

When your teacher gives you a test in school, he or she wants to know what you know. But when your boss gives you an assignment at work, he or she wants to know what you'll do with what you've learned.

Let's play a game of Simon Says. We all know we're supposed to move only when we hear the words "Simon says." Listening to instructions is one thing, but we also need to wisely carry them out. Whoever shows the most wisdom wins the game.

WISDOM

SCRIPTURE READING: PROVERBS 1:1–7

What does the Bible have to say on the subject of wisdom? A lot! Let's dive in.

Happy is a man who finds wisdom and who acquires understanding.
PROVERBS 3:13

A fool's way is right in his own eyes, but whoever listens to counsel is wise. PROVERBS 12:15

A wise man is cautious and turns from evil, but a fool is easily angered and is careless. PROVERBS 14:16

The mind of the discerning acquires knowledge, and the ear of the wise seeks it. PROVERBS 18:15

Who is like the wise person, and who knows the interpretation of a matter? A man's wisdom brightens his face, and the sternness of his face is changed. ECCLESIASTES 8:1

I [God] will give you such words and a wisdom that none of your adversaries will be able to resist or contradict. LUKE 21:15

Pay careful attention, then, to how you walk—not as unwise people but as wise. EPHESIANS 5:15

If any of you lacks wisdom, he should ask God, who gives to all generously and without criticizing, and it will be given to him.
JAMES 1:5

The wisdom from above is first pure, then peace-loving, gentle, compliant, full of mercy and good fruits, without favoritism and hypocrisy. JAMES 3:17

That's a lot to think about! Let's discuss what these passages mean to us and how we can apply them in our own lives.

WISDOM

Scripture Reading: Ecclesiastes 7:19

It's always a good idea if two teams prepare before they face each other in a sports competition. Some teams prepare by watching film of the other team playing. This game film shows what the other team did really well and how to best prepare to play them.

Knowledge without execution is meaningless in a sporting game, but knowledge with execution generates big plays and a greater chance of winning. The reality is, no matter how much studying each team does to know their game plan, their only chance of winning is to execute what they know.

The same is true with our knowledge of the Bible. It becomes wisdom when we apply what we know. When we use it and do it.

(Use a large piece of paper for this activity.) To illustrate this point, let's do an activity. We'll make two columns on this paper. The column on the left will be labeled "Biblical Knowledge." The column on the right will be labeled "Application of Wisdom." In the "Biblical Knowledge" column, we'll list a principle from the Bible, such as "Love one another." Then in the "Application of Wisdom" column, we'll write down what it means to apply that principle in our daily lives. *(See the following example.)*

Let's brainstorm at least six ideas for each column.

BIBLICAL KNOWLEDGE	APPLICATION OF WISDOM
Love one another.	Carry the grocery bags for Mom from the car to the house without her asking.

WISDOM

SCRIPTURE READING: EPHESIANS 5:15–17

Have you ever played a video game and made a bad choice? Maybe you went left when you should have gone right. Or you jumped when you should have run. Or talked back to someone when you shouldn't have.

Have you ever played a video game and faced the enemy when you weren't prepared to win? When that happens in a video game, your character, car, contraption, or whatever it is that you're controlling usually zaps, poofs, and disappears. You definitely don't get to move forward. In fact, sometimes you end up having to start all over again. Right?

In life (thankfully) you don't get zapped—or poof and disappear—when you make unwise choices. But your bad choices can set you back in other ways. They can

- ruin a relationship,
- cause you to do poorly on a school assignment,
- mess up your health, or
- get you grounded or in trouble at home.

Whatever the situation is, unwise choices stop you from moving forward. Wisdom is just as important in life as it is when you're playing video games.

For Fun Friday, let's choose a video game, a game on a smartphone or tablet, or even a board game to play. *(As you play, discuss the importance of making wise choices in the game and in life.)*

Let's close in prayer, asking God to help us make wise choices.

HUMILITY

SCRIPTURE READING: PHILIPPIANS 2:3

Think of a time when you've been wrong or done something wrong. Maybe you were wrong in the way you treated someone. Or you didn't obey us because you were having too much fun playing, or you just didn't feel like it. It could be that you said some unkind words to someone or felt jealous or prideful.

It's okay. You aren't going to get in trouble. Let's all share one time when we were wrong.

After we're done sharing, we'll each apologize for whatever we did that was wrong. Why? Because apologizing shows humility. And God wants us to be humble, because when we're humble, we're honest.

Everyone has done wrong things. But a proud person won't admit it very easily and will definitely not apologize. So let's practice apologizing right now.

When you apologize, you don't need to put yourself down. You're a valuable child of the King! But you can apologize for doing something wrong, especially if it hurt or disappointed someone. If it didn't affect anyone in our family, go ahead and apologize anyway, because we love you and want to see you be your best.

Learning to apologize whenever you're wrong is a great way to stay humble!

HUMILITY

SCRIPTURE READING: JAMES 4:6

This week we're learning about humility. Humility is the opposite of pride. When we're humble, we're willing to listen to God and do what He says—even when we think we have a better way. To think our way is better than God's way means that we're prideful, not humble. Since God knows everything, we should humble ourselves and follow His guidance.

Jesus Christ showed us what it means to be humble. Even though He was the Son of God, He submitted Himself to the will of His Father. He even died on the cross because it was part of God's plan. If Jesus submitted Himself to God, shouldn't we?

Let's talk about how we can learn to be humble. *(Allow time for everyone to contribute to the discussion.)*

In what areas of your life are you doing things your way instead of God's way? In what areas of your life can you work harder to be humble even though it may hurt or be a struggle? How can you practice being humble in our family? How can you be a better listener? How can you put others ahead of yourself?

Let's pray together and ask God to help each of us practice humility, even when it's difficult.

HUMILITY

SCRIPTURE READING: LUKE 14:11

You might not be surprised to hear that the Bible has a lot to say about the subject of humility. For today's Wednesday in the Word, let's find out more about this important topic.

The result of humility is fear of the LORD, along with wealth, honor, and life. PROVERBS 22:4

Everyone who exalts himself will be humbled, and the one who humbles himself will be exalted. LUKE 14:11

By the grace given to me, I tell everyone among you not to think of himself more highly than he should think. Instead, think sensibly, as God has distributed a measure of faith to each one. ROMANS 12:3

Do nothing out of rivalry or conceit, but in humility consider others as more important than yourselves. PHILIPPIANS 2:3

Therefore, God's chosen ones, holy and loved, put on heartfelt compassion, kindness, humility, gentleness, and patience. COLOSSIANS 3:12

[The Holy Spirit] gives greater grace. Therefore He says: God resists the proud, but gives grace to the humble. JAMES 4:6

Humble yourselves, therefore, under the mighty hand of God, so that He may exalt you at the proper time. 1 PETER 5:6

That's just the beginning of what God has to say about humility. God feels very strongly about this area, doesn't He? And because He does, we should too.

What are some ways you can develop a humble heart before the Lord?

HUMILITY

SCRIPTURE READING: PROVERBS 22:4

Humility is the willingness to be coachable. It means you feel that you always have the ability to grow and become more like Jesus. There are always people who are prideful and think they've already made it in life. They aren't willing to allow others to disciple them. What those Christians don't realize is that by not being humble, they've limited their ability to grow stronger in the Lord.

God is always looking for humble people. His eyes are on those who humble themselves before Him. As we saw yesterday, God says He will "exalt" or lift up the humble and give them honor. Let's read James 4:10 aloud.

We're to be humble because God is truly greater than all of us. Let's play a game called Power Struggle to remind us of His greatness. One person starts a rhyme, and the others respond together. Here's the rhyme:

There once was a flea who spoke right out loud,
"I'm so big! I'm so big! I'm as big as that cloud!"

[Others respond:] "Hey, little buddy," said God with a wink,
"You're really not quite as big as you think!
I hate to disappoint you, but I have a strong hunch,
There are quite a few others who could eat you for lunch!"

Now repeat the rhyme, but replace the flea with a slightly bigger bug or animal. Keep repeating the rhyme, replacing the bug or animal with an even bigger one, until you get to the biggest creature you can think of—like a whale.

This game helps us see that no matter how "big" we are on Earth, God is always bigger!

HUMILITY

SCRIPTURE READING: 1 PETER 5:6

There's nothing like a good dose of humility to cure the sin of pride! To illustrate, let me tell you a story. An army colonel had just received his promotion and was feeling pretty good about himself. He was sitting at his desk when someone knocked at his office door and said, "This is Private Johnson. May I see you, sir?"

Instead of inviting the soldier in, the colonel said, "Just a minute." Then, to look impressive, he picked up his telephone and said loudly, "Yes, Mr. President. I understand, Mr. President. I'll take care of it right away, Mr. President."

He wasn't talking to the president, but he wanted to make it seem as if he was. He wanted to appear bigger and more important than he really was.

The colonel said, "Mr. President, just give me one second." Then he said, "Come in, Private."

The private came in, and the colonel asked, "What can I do for you? Make it quick!"

"Well," the private said, "I just came in to connect your telephone."

When we forget about humility, like the colonel, God has a way of making us look foolish. Proverbs 16:18 tells us that "pride comes before destruction, and an arrogant spirit before a fall."

Often, our family and friends can tell when we're acting out of pride. Let's come up with some ideas for how they could bring it to our attention.

215

SUCCESS

SCRIPTURE READING: PHILIPPIANS 4:13

Jesus didn't live a long time on Earth—just thirty-three years—but He lived a very full and successful life. He prayed to His Father in John 17, "I finished the work You sent Me here to do" (verse 4, author paraphrase).

There's no greater statement you can make at the end of your life than saying you finished what you were put on this earth to do. That's a successful life. When you have no sense that you're accomplishing God's purpose for your life, then, of course, something is missing or wrong.

Jesus lived a very successful life. The secret of His life and success was His communion with the Father. Jesus spent a great deal of time alone with God, and God empowered His Son to do great works in a short time.

For example, when Jesus performed a miracle, he would speak, and the miracle would happen in only a few seconds. This was possible only because He had spent extraordinary time with God.

To live successful lives, we need to increase the amount of time we spend with God. When we do, we'll receive His power and wisdom to carry out His plan for our lives.

How much time do you spend with God each day? What does it look like to spend time with God?

SUCCESS

SCRIPTURE READING: PROVERBS 16:3

This week we're learning about true success. *Success* can be defined as "finding, understanding, and expressing the purposes of God in our lives." We can appear unsuccessful in the world but still be very successful in the kingdom of God.

Human beings define *success* very differently than God does. Success according to the Bible isn't based on riches, power, looks, or material things. It refers to displaying the image of God in our lives. God created us in His image and wants us to display His image in all we do. If we don't express the image of God, we might appear to be successful to the world and yet not be successful at all.

Let's talk about how each of us defines *success*. How do you feel most people define it? When you think of being successful, what does that look like for you? What's a poor definition of *success*? What do you think you can do to be more successful in the kingdom of God instead of in the world?

Let's pray and ask God to teach us the real meaning of success as we follow Him.

SUCCESS

SCRIPTURE READING: JAMES 1:25

John 5:19 gives us the secret to success. In the words of Jesus, "I assure you: The Son is not able to do anything on His own, but only what He sees the Father doing. For whatever the Father does, the Son also does these things in the same way."

Jesus did only what He saw His Father doing. He didn't just come up with stuff to do or decide on His own what He would do. He looked to see what His Father was doing and then joined in to accomplish His Father's kingdom agenda. Now that's a no-lose deal. God is already doing something in the world, and all we need to do is merge into it. His agenda has to work because God is perfect.

Jesus spent time with God on a regular and ongoing basis. The Father was Jesus' source and guide in everything. In order for us to truly be successful, God needs to be our source and guide as well, each and every day.

For today's Wednesday in the Word, we'll use the online search feature on a computer, smartphone, or tablet to look up Bible verses on different topics. This is a great way to find out what God says about many important subjects. Let's each come up with two or three Bible verses and read them aloud. The topics for your online search are . . .

1. Giving to others
2. Loving others
3. Obeying your parents
4. Helping the poor
5. Controlling pride

Let's pray together and thank God for showing us how to be successful in all areas of life.

SUCCESS

SCRIPTURE READING: PSALM 37:4

Big Ben is a famous tower clock in London; it towers high above people, cars, and buildings. People often walk past Big Ben and check the time to see whether their own watches are correct. If your watch doesn't match Big Ben, you wouldn't try to change Big Ben, would you? Instead, you'd change your own watch to match Big Ben.

Big Ben is the standard for the correct time, so to be correct, all other timepieces need to be in sync with Big Ben.

In a similar way, Jesus Christ should be the focus of all Christians around the world. He sits on His heavenly throne as king and is the source of true life and success for every believer. If we aren't checking with Jesus to line up with His standard, we may be living but not living successfully.

Jesus, not the world, defines success.

For today's activity, each of us will draw on a tablet or a piece of paper something Jesus Christ would say is a successful thing to do. It could be serving the poor, taking a missions trip, or helping an elderly person clean his or her yard. You decide what to draw, but choose something that reflects Jesus' standard of success.

Then we'll go around the room, and each of us will talk about our drawings and why we chose them.

SUCCESS

SCRIPTURE READING: PROVERBS 3:1–4

Did you know that obedience is very important when it comes to success? Today's Fun Friday activity will illustrate this truth for all of us.

(For this activity, you'll need some dirty pennies, two small bowls, salt, vinegar, and cotton swabs.) We're going to clean pennies with vinegar. I'll drop some pennies in a bowl; then each of us will dip a cotton swab in the vinegar and start scrubbing. Scrub your penny as hard as you can!

Did you notice that the vinegar cleans the pennies a little, but not a lot? That's disappointing, isn't it? The vinegar should have cleaned better than that. Let's go back and read the instructions. Something was missing. This time we're going to mix some salt in the vinegar!

Now I need a volunteer to stir one teaspoon of salt into one-fourth cup of vinegar. Stir in the salt until it's dissolved. Then we'll drop the pennies in the mixture and stir a little bit more. Now we have clean pennies!

Just as following the instructions was important for success in cleaning those pennies, following God's Word and His guidance is important for success in life.

COURTEOUS SPEECH

SCRIPTURE READING: PROVERBS 16:24

God's Word tells us, "Those who guard their lips preserve their lives, but those who speak rashly will come to ruin" (Proverbs 13:3, NIV).

What does it mean to "speak rashly"?

Does everything that comes to your mind need to come out of your mouth? How can you choose what should come out of your mouth?

Should you speak words that will hurt others? Why or why not?

Let's ask God to help us with our mouths so that we might speak courteously to others. Here are some prayers we might pray:

Dear God, please help me guard my mouth and what I say (Proverbs 13:3).

Dear God, I feel very hurt and angry. Please help my heart to be right, and keep me from saying anything I'll regret.

Dear God, please watch over my thoughts and the words that come out of my mouth so I don't say things to make others feel bad. Instead, help me think of encouraging and helpful things to say (Psalm 141:3).

COURTEOUS SPEECH

SCRIPTURE READING: PROVERBS 15:1

God loves it when we say positive things to build each other up. We must never use speech that tears others down or discourages them. Instead, we should always try to choose words that are positive, encouraging, and uplifting.

God says in His Word, "Do not let any unwholesome talk come out of your mouths, but only what is helpful for building others up according to their needs, that it may benefit those who listen" (Ephesians 4:29, NIV).

To create a reminder of this very important principle, let's build a house! We can choose to use building blocks, bricks, sugar cubes, or other creative building materials. Every time someone in our family says something positive that builds up another person in our home, he or she will receive a block, a brick, a sugar cube, or something else. As each of us collects more building materials, we'll use them to build a house.

Let's try to speak as many positive words as possible this week. Just remember, if you use a negative, destructive word, you'll lose one of your building supplies. By the end of the day on Friday, we'll see who can build the biggest house.

This activity will help us remember that whenever we do something good for the Lord here on Earth, we're storing up building materials for our reward in heaven someday.

COURTEOUS SPEECH

SCRIPTURE READING: EPHESIANS 4:29

God has plenty to say about using courteous speech. Let's dive right in.

A gentle answer turns away anger, but a harsh word stirs up wrath.
PROVERBS 15:1

The tongue that heals is a tree of life, but a devious tongue breaks the spirit. PROVERBS 15:4

Pleasant words are a honeycomb: sweet to the taste and health to the body. PROVERBS 16:24

The intelligent person restrains his words, and one who keeps a cool head is a man of understanding. PROVERBS 17:27

The one who gives an answer before he listens—this is foolishness and disgrace for him. PROVERBS 18:13

To remind us how important it is to use our mouths for good, not harm, let's agree to hold one another accountable for our speech. Whenever a family member says something negative, harsh, or hurtful during our times together, that person will be asked to do a quick chore. It might be something like taking out the trash or cleaning the toilet.

It makes a difference when immediate consequences are tied to our words, doesn't it?

Let's close in prayer, asking God to make us aware of the power of our words and the need to use them for His glory and the good of others.

COURTEOUS SPEECH

SCRIPTURE READING: 1 THESSALONIANS 5:11

Let's read James 1:19–20 together, and then we'll talk about how we use our words to express our feelings. "My dearly loved brothers, understand this: Everyone must be quick to hear, slow to speak, and slow to anger, for man's anger does not accomplish God's righteousness."

How do you feel when you get upset? Is it easy or hard to control your emotions? Do you want to talk when you're upset?

What is the first thing many people do when they get angry? Do the words they say when they're mad usually bring about a good result or a bad one?

What does this verse say we should be slow to do? Why do you think it's a good idea to be slow to get angry and slow to speak harsh words?

Have you ever squeezed toothpaste out of a toothpaste container and then tried to put it back in? It won't go back in, will it? That's how it is with the words we speak. Once we say them, even if we wish we hadn't, we can't take them back. That's why it's very important to follow the wisdom of these verses.

Let's pray together, thanking God that He is there to help us control our words, even when we are angry.

COURTEOUS SPEECH

SCRIPTURE READING: PROVERBS 25:11

Our speech is important, of course. It's also important that our speech matches our actions. It's confusing if people say one thing but do another, isn't it?

For today's Fun Friday activity, let's play a matching game. We'll cut different shapes out of paper and then each of us will take a turn matching shapes together. We'll need to cut out two squares, two circles, two rectangles, and two of any other shape we make. This activity reminds us that our words need to match our actions. For example, if you say "I love you" to your sister or brother but don't share your game or your toy with him or her, are your words matching your actions?

Can you give other examples of when our words don't match our actions? *(Encourage responses and share your own ideas too.)* Now give some examples of when they do.

Courteous speech should always be paired with courteous actions. God wants our hearts, our mouths, and our hands to reflect His love. Let's be sure to keep this in mind whenever we speak and act.

Let's pray and ask God to help us practice courteous speech and behavior.

IDENTITY

SCRIPTURE READING: GENESIS 1:27

Your identity is who you are. It isn't what you do. Sometimes what you do can influence your identity and reflect it, but ultimately your identity is who you are. It reflects your personality and your character—everything that's unique about you. Just as no one else has the same fingerprints you do, no one else shares your identity. You are *unique*. You are *rare*. And you are *valuable*.

Your identity includes all of you. You aren't just a head. You aren't just arms. You aren't just your thoughts. If you built a character for a video game and didn't include all of the pieces of the body, you'd have a zombie or a monster, right? When you build a character to play in a game, you have to include all the body parts before you can move to the next level.

Your identity might have some painful aspects to it, but God can teach you valuable lessons and make you stronger through your struggles *if* you let Him.

Grow through your pain and weaknesses. Maximize and feed your strengths. Allow for your uniqueness. When you do that, God will mix it all together so you'll have a strong identity.

Today we're going to draw characters for a video game that will represent each of us. Your character should be a picture of who you are (your identity), so be sure to include the different character qualities, gifts, and interests you have, not just how you look. If you enjoy reading, put a book in your hand. If you're great at soccer, put a ball by your foot (or on your head). If God has been teaching you how to love others, draw a heart. If you're good at encouraging others, draw yourself giving someone a hug. You get the point. When everyone is done, we'll talk about our identity pictures and why we chose the qualities we did.

IDENTITY

SCRIPTURE READING: JEREMIAH 1:5

This week we're learning about identity. Understanding your identity is extremely important if you want to fulfill God's purposes for your life.

When people are unsure of their identities, the culture or other people can easily influence them. People often search for an identity in all the wrong places. The Bible says that our true identities are found in Christ.

Think of it like this: Every toy gets its identity from the person or company who made it. It seems right that whoever makes a product gives it an identity.

The one who created you gave you your identity. Don't try looking to other people to find out who you are, because they didn't create you. God did! Find your identity in Him.

For today's activity, let's pretend we're strangers and introduce ourselves to each other. Everyone take a turn. State your whole name, where you're from, and when your birthday is. Then declare that you're a child of God. Remember, your true identity is found only in Him!

Let's pray and ask God to help us understand our identity in Him and reveal His plan for our lives.

IDENTITY

SCRIPTURE READING: 2 CORINTHIANS 5:17

Let's read and discuss two Bible verses about identity for today's Wednesday in the Word.

We are [God's] creation, created in Christ Jesus for good works, which God prepared ahead of time so that we should walk in them.
EPHESIANS 2:10

Why did God create you? What good works does He have for you to do?

You are a chosen race, a royal priesthood, a holy nation, a people for His possession, so that you may proclaim the praises of the One who called you out of darkness into His marvelous light. 1 PETER 2:9

How does it feel to know that you're God's treasured possession? What do you think it means to be called out of darkness into God's light?

It's great to memorize Scripture. This way it gets into our hearts and our spirits. One way to do that is to repeat a passage over and over. Another way is to write it down. A third way is to text it to someone.

Let's have a texting competition and see who can text these two Scriptures the fastest (without making any mistakes). *(Younger kids can pair up with an older partner. If someone is too young for this activity, have him or her repeat the words before you push Send.)*

Let's try this competition a few times in different ways and with different teams. Before we know it, we'll have these two verses memorized!

IDENTITY

SCRIPTURE READING: 1 PETER 2:9

X-Men was a blockbuster movie based on a series of comic books about mutants taking over the world. Some of the mutants were good, and some were bad. Whether good or bad, all of them had special powers. One of the characters, Storm, could control the weather; Xavier could control minds. Wolverine had the ability to heal instantly, and Cyclops could burn things with his eyes.

Mystique had the power of identity. She could change her appearance to blend in with her environment. One minute she could be Mystique, and the next she could turn herself into the president of the United States. Her identity was always changing, so people were confused about who she really was. Was she good or evil? It turned out that Mystique was a villain who caused conflict and trouble for the good guys in the film.*

Some people are too much like Mystique when it comes to their identities. They shift and change to blend in with whatever environment they're in. Some kids ignore who they are to get their friends to like them more. Some are more concerned with fitting in with the culture than they are with being who God created them to be. When you know who you are in Christ, you don't feel the need to change your true identity just to blend in. Jesus Christ has made you unique, one of a kind, and special.

Talk about a time when you changed your identity to try to fit in. How did that make you feel?

Let's thank God for making each of us special and ask Him to help us use our individual strengths to show His love to the world.

---

* *X-Men*, directed by Bryan Singer (Los Angeles: Twentieth Century Fox, 2000).

IDENTITY

SCRIPTURE READING: 1 CORINTHIANS 12:27

It's baking day! But before we bake something for Fun Friday, I have a few questions for you.

Have you ever gone to the kitchen after a batch of cookies or a cake was put in the oven and licked out the bowl? Or have you ever grabbed the spatula from a family member before he or she could lick it first? How about opening up a ready-made cookie roll before it's baked and eating a spoonful or two?

Most people love cookie dough. In fact, they love it so much that manufacturers now include it in ice cream and milk shakes.

But have you ever been tempted to lick the bowl when the eggs and salt were being mixed together? Probably not. Or have you ever wanted to grab the baking soda and dump a spoonful into your mouth? Have you ever snuck into the kitchen after everyone has gone to bed and swiped a stick of butter? Have you ever quietly lifted the lid off the flour container so that no one would hear you, and you wouldn't get caught eating raw flour with a spoon? Probably not!

That's because none of these ingredients taste good alone. Butter by itself tastes nasty. Baking soda by itself is bitter. Flour by itself tastes dry. And raw eggs aren't very appetizing. By themselves, none of those ingredients would tempt your taste buds, right? Yet when someone steps into the kitchen and mixes them all together for an intended purpose, they are *really* good.

God has a purpose for you, and He uses all the ingredients in your life to make up your identity—even the hard things. Trust Him. He's making you into something great!

Now let's go and bake something special. While we do, we can talk about what we learned today.

TEMPTATION

SCRIPTURE READING: 1 CORINTHIANS 10:13

A businessman was on a diet when he suddenly had a craving for donuts. He drove to the donut shop, but there were no parking spaces. So he just kept circling the block. Finally he prayed, *Lord, I know You don't want me to eat donuts. I know that's not Your will, but I need You to confirm it. There are no parking spaces at this donut shop, so I'm going to drive around the block again. If no parking space opens up, that will serve as confirmation.*

After he drove around the block *eight* more times, a spot finally became available!

How did this businessman handle the temptation to go off his diet and eat donuts? What position did he put himself in—a position to overcome his craving or find a way to satisfy it?

There's nothing spiritually wrong with donuts. This is just a story to illustrate the importance of setting up boundaries when we feel drawn to do something we know we shouldn't be doing. For the man in the story, driving around the donut shop eight more times wasn't setting up a real boundary.

What are some things he could have done that might have helped him overcome his temptation to eat a donut? List some reasons he failed to resist this temptation. What are some things you can do to resist doing what you shouldn't do?

Temptation by itself isn't sin. It's what comes before a decision to sin. Whenever we're tempted, God gives us a window of time to choose to do what's right instead of what's wrong.

Let's pray together and ask God to help us understand temptation so we can make better decisions each day.

TEMPTATION

SCRIPTURE READING: MATTHEW 26:41

This week we're learning about temptation. That's the strong feeling of being pulled to do something we know we shouldn't do. For instance, when you've been told you can't eat any cookies from the cookie jar, but you feel as if the cookies are calling your name, you're experiencing temptation. The cookies keep calling to you, so you give in and eat one. Or three.

Everyone has experienced and will continue to experience temptation. The question isn't "Will we be tempted?" The question is "What will we do when temptation comes?" As we get older, temptations don't get easier to handle; they just get bigger. So it's important to learn how to handle temptation now and practice doing what's right when it's telling you to do what's wrong.

Let's talk about times in our lives when we've been tempted. Share a story of a time you gave in to temptation and a time you overcame it. What helped you win the battle?

Now let's pray together and ask God to strengthen us and teach us how to overcome temptation when it comes our way.

TEMPTATION

SCRIPTURE READING: JAMES 4:7

Winning the battle with temptation usually isn't a onetime deal. It's often an ongoing process of leaning on God's strength so we can make the right choice whenever we're faced with the wrong choice.

Let's look at some Bible verses for today's Wednesday in the Word. After we read each verse, we'll talk about what it means.

No temptation has overtaken you but such as is common to man; and God is faithful, who will not allow you to be tempted beyond what you are able, but with the temptation will provide the way of escape also, so that you will be able to endure it.
I CORINTHIANS 10:13, NASB

We do not have a high priest who cannot sympathize with our weaknesses, but One who has been tempted in all things as we are, yet without sin. Therefore let us draw near with confidence to the throne of grace, so that we may receive mercy and find grace to help in time of need. HEBREWS 4:15–16, NASB

Each one is tempted when he is carried away and enticed by his own lust. JAMES 1:14, NASB

Submit therefore to God. Resist the devil and he will flee from you.
JAMES 4:7, NASB

How does God help us through tempting times? Let's each share one way that He has helped us when we've been tempted in the past. Then let's pray together, asking for His strength to overcome temptation in the future.

TEMPTATION

SCRIPTURE READING: HEBREWS 2:18

There are lots of situations in life that tempt us to cheat to get ahead. Whether it's cheating to pass a test, cheating to win a game, or lying to avoid getting in trouble, we're all susceptible to temptation.

There will be times in life when you'll be tempted to do the wrong thing so you can move in the right direction. But the true winners in the Christian life are those who become successful by following God's rules.

Remember, the question is "What will you do when temptation comes?"

Temptation will try to convince you to move when you should stop. It will try to get you to lie when you should tell the truth. It will try to get you to do things your own way when you should do things God's way. The true winners in the game of life are those who learn to stand strong against temptation.

(For today's activity, prepare a tasty dessert or candy treat ahead of time. Put it on the table during your mealtime or have it in sight during your family time.)

You've probably noticed the treat sitting on the table.

Even though you're welcome to enjoy it after the meal or during our lesson, it would be good if you'd practice saying no to your desires. Learning how to resist temptation now will help you stand strong in the future. But it's your choice.

After you make your decision about whether to eat the treat, talk about how you feel.

TEMPTATION

SCRIPTURE READING: MARK 14:38

Focusing on your sin to get rid of it is as successful as a person on a diet focusing on a Pizza Hut menu to understand what to avoid. It's counterproductive. If you know you need to stay away from pizza, you shouldn't study Pizza Hut menus. It will only make you hungrier for things you're trying to stay away from.

Instead of focusing on what you're doing wrong or what you're trying to avoid, work to change your mind-set and focus on good choices you can make instead. Let your mind dwell on what is pure, right, lovely, and true (Philippians 4:8). When you do that, you'll find you have the ability to overcome sin and temptation. This is because we often do what we think about.

Today we're going to come up with a creative strategy to overcome temptation. Maybe you're tempted to talk back to us when we ask you to take out the trash or clean your room. Let's come up with a creative way to change the way you view these chores and communicate with us so you'll respond more naturally in the right way.

Since this is Fun Friday, let's play a fun role-playing game so you can practice your strategy. First, we'll make a list of situations we run into here at home. Then we'll choose one situation, and one person will play the parent's role, and the other will act out the right way to respond. Or we can start with acting out the wrong way to respond, followed by the right way!

(After you've talked about responding the right way to temptation, go around the room and pray for each family member, asking God to strengthen him or her. Remember that prayer goes a long way in giving us the power to overcome temptation.)

MATURITY

SCRIPTURE READING: 1 CORINTHIANS 14:20

*S*piritual maturity can simply be defined as "more of Jesus being expressed in my life through less of me." We all want to grow to be more like Jesus, setting aside our own selfish interests to make His character our own.

The stages of your spiritual life are similar to the way you grow up physically, starting with childhood, moving through the teenage years, and ending up in adulthood.

Each of these stages is important. Is any baby born an adult? No. That would be funny, wouldn't it? Adults can't skip their teen years. And teens can't skip their childhood years.

God's Word encourages us to keep growing. We're to "[leave] the elementary teaching about the Christ [and] press on to maturity, not laying again a foundation of repentance from dead works and of faith toward God" (Hebrews 6:1, NASB).

But there's a problem when Christians get stuck along the way, and their spiritual growth never matures. The Bible says,

> *Though by this time you ought to be teachers, you have need again for someone to teach you . . . , and you have come to need milk and not solid food. For everyone who partakes only of milk is not accustomed to the word of righteousness, for he is an infant. But solid food is for the mature, who because of practice have their senses trained to discern good and evil.* HEBREWS 5:12–14, NASB

Let's talk about this passage and what it means for our lives. How would you define *spiritual maturity* in your own words? What does it mean to need milk and not solid food? What is the connection between our obedience and spiritual maturity?

MATURITY

SCRIPTURE READING: 1 CORINTHIANS 13:11

This week we're learning about maturity. Maturity involves growing from childhood to adulthood. To put it another way, maturity is moving from unripe to ripe. No one wants to eat fruit that isn't ripe yet; it can taste sour or bland.

Much like fruit, people go through a process of becoming ripe or mature. This doesn't mean that you simply get bigger physically; it means that you become ripe spiritually, emotionally, and mentally. That is, you can look like an adult and be spiritually immature, or you can be young and yet be spiritually mature.

Let's take a short quiz to gauge our maturity.

1. Are you always seeking to learn? Or do you think you already know everything? *(Explain that those who are willing to learn show signs of being ripe. It's hard to learn when you think you don't need to.)*

2. Is your identity focused on Christ? Or is your identity focused on people and material things? *(Explain that spiritual maturity is understanding who you are in Christ, not changing with the wind of public opinion.)*

3. Do you easily give in to temptation? *(Note that a sign of being mature is not giving in to something you know isn't right.)*

Let's pray together and thank God that He is helping us become spiritually mature as we learn about Him and follow Him.

MATURITY

SCRIPTURE READING: EPHESIANS 4:14–15

One day a homeowner walked through his yard with a workman who was helping cut down and remove dead trees. The homeowner showed the workman one tree that looked dead and asked that the tree be cut down.

"Oh, sir," said the workman, "you don't need to cut this tree down. It's still alive." Then he pointed out some small green buds on the tree that were barely visible. What looked like a dead tree was really stunted growth. Because this tree hadn't been properly nurtured and developed, it appeared to have no life at all.

Some Christians today are like that underdeveloped tree. There's life, but they're not experiencing the abundant life Jesus promised because they lack growth.

Let's look at some Scripture passages on spiritual growth for today's Wednesday in the Word:

Bring my sons from afar and my daughters from the ends of the earth, everyone who is called by My name, and whom I have created for My glory, whom I have formed, even whom I have made. ISAIAH 43:6–7, NASB

Why were you created?

Like newborn babies, crave pure spiritual milk, so that by it you may grow up in your salvation. 1 PETER 2:2, NIV

What is the true goal of spiritual growth?

Let's close in prayer, asking God to help us grow spiritually so we can reveal His glory to the world.

MATURITY

SCRIPTURE READING: HEBREWS 6:1–3

When bananas first grow, they're green instead of yellow. Green bananas aren't useful because they aren't ripe yet. If you try to peel and eat a green banana, not only will it be hard to peel; it also won't be good to eat.

Eating a banana that isn't ripe is a miserable experience. A banana has the potential to be a tasty, sweet fruit that can be used many different ways. You can eat bananas in ice-cream sundaes, smoothies, banana pudding, banana bread, and more. What's your favorite way to eat a banana?

Imagine eating a green banana. *(You may want to buy green bananas in preparation for today's devotional and slice up small bites for everyone to try.)*

Is it sweet or bitter? When the banana turns yellow, it's letting you know that it's ready to eat. It is now mature.

Reaching maturity in life is the process of becoming physically, spiritually, mentally, and emotionally ripe. If a person is still green, he or she hasn't matured. That person hasn't learned to make good decisions or put God first in everything or avoid being selfish. He or she is bitter rather than sweet.

God wants us to be mature and show His love to others. Can you list some traits of an immature believer? Let's work together to create a list.

Now let's list some traits of a mature believer.

Think about yourself now. Which list describes you best? Which traits do you want to have?

Let's close in prayer and ask God to help us to grow in Him every day.

MATURITY

SCRIPTURE READING: EPHESIANS 4:13

The apostle Paul issued this challenge to the Corinthians: "Do not be children in your thinking; yet in evil be infants, but in your thinking be mature" (1 Corinthians 14:20, NASB).

Spiritual maturity is the ability to consistently view and live life from the perspective of the Holy Spirit rather than the flesh, with the result that we maximize our God-given capacity to bring Him glory.

Spiritual maturity is something we'll be pursuing all of our lives, because we'll never do it perfectly here on Earth. There will always be room for more growth.

Do you know anyone who is elderly? This week for Fun Friday, let's write or create cards to thank an elderly person we know for all the ways he or she has served the Lord in life. That person might be a relative or another elderly person you know.

This activity is intended to remind us that we're always growing and never truly reach the final stage of maturity.

Be sure to mail your card or take it to the person you've chosen. Let that person know how much you respect and love him or her.

JESUS CHRIST

SCRIPTURE READING: JOHN 14:6

Jesus Christ is fully God. He also came to Earth as a human being. He was no less God when He became human. Mary didn't give birth to both God and man. Jesus wasn't 50 percent human and 50 percent God. When she gave birth to Jesus, He was fully God and fully man at the same time. Jesus was born of God so that He might be God with us—Immanuel. The name *Immanuel* literally means "God with us." We read in Colossians 1:19 that "God was pleased to have all His fullness dwell in [Christ]."

Jesus Christ is different from God the Father in His personhood, and yet He's equal with God in His deity. He took on human flesh, being born as a baby in a world of darkness. He came for the purpose of making the invisible God visible to us.

Jesus came to Earth not only to be the perfect sacrifice and atonement for our sins but also so that we might have an idea of what God looks like. He is the exact representation of God in the flesh. By learning about the life of Jesus, we learn about God—because Jesus is God.

Today we'll look at how we can blend two things together and make them wholly one. *(For this activity, you'll need a glass and some food coloring.)* Watch what happens when I put a couple of drops of food coloring in a glass of water. You can see that the food coloring isn't water and the water isn't food coloring. But as soon as we put a couple of drops of food coloring into the water, the water takes on that color completely. *(Stir the water and talk about what happens.)*

Is the liquid 50 percent food coloring? *(No.)* Is it 50 percent water? *(No.)* It's 100 percent blended together.

This is a great illustration of what happened when Jesus became a human being. He didn't stop being God. He is fully God and fully human.

JESUS CHRIST

Scripture Reading: 1 Timothy 2:5

This week we're studying the most important topic of all: the person of Jesus Christ. Jesus is God and man all at the same time.

To understand what it means for Jesus to be God and man, think of your favorite superhero. Maybe you like Superman, Spider-Man, Batman, or Wonder Woman. All superheroes have something in common. They have special powers beyond those of regular human beings, and they can save people because of these special powers. In the same way, Jesus had the power of God while He also lived as a human being. Because He is God, He can save you from your sins. Because He became human, He understands what it's like to be human. He also has the ability to relate to you as a person.

We must understand that Jesus Christ is greater than the greatest superhero of all time. Superman can save people for a moment, but Jesus can save people forever.

Let's talk about our favorite superheroes. What are the special powers of your favorite superhero? How did he or she get the power to do all of those things? What are the special powers of Jesus Christ? Where did His power come from?

Let's pray and thank God for sending His only Son, Jesus, who has the power to save us for all eternity.

JESUS CHRIST

SCRIPTURE READING: ACTS 4:11–12

You have "a friend who sticks closer than a brother" (Proverbs 18:24, NIV). That friend is your savior, Jesus Christ. He's your friend because He is fully human. He's your savior because He is fully God.

We can expect bad days. They come with living here on Earth, where people make mistakes and poor decisions. But we also have a great source of peace, happiness, and courage—our friend and savior, Jesus Christ. In fact, He's the only true source of these things. Jesus clearly said, "I have told you these things so that in Me you may have peace. You will have suffering in this world. Be courageous! I have conquered the world" (John 16:33).

Jesus has that kind of power. One example is when He calmed the waves when He and His disciples were on the sea in a storm. Now that's power! Maybe He told them something like, "On the sea you'll have fierce winds and wicked waves, but don't be afraid, I will calm the storm."

Let's name some other things Jesus did to bring peace to people. Did He heal? Did He comfort anyone? When? *(If family members have difficulty thinking of examples, give them some hints.)*

For today's Wednesday in the Word, let's memorize John 16:33 by turning it into a catchy song.

We all face uneasy times. We all have bad days. We all face situations where things seem out of our control. But Jesus has power over everything. We can access His power when we spend time with Him and put our trust in Him.

JESUS CHRIST

SCRIPTURE READING: HEBREWS 13:8

Superman is one of the most powerful superheroes in the history of comic books. Because he's super, he can do extraordinary things that regular people can't do. Because he's also a man, he can do things that regular people can also do. This is why he's called Superman.

Jesus Christ is the real Superman. When He was on Earth, He could do extraordinary things that regular people couldn't do. And because He was also a man, He could do all of the regular things that every regular person could do. Jesus Christ was the God-man.

One minute He could walk on water because He was God, and the next minute He could be thirsty because He was a man. As a man He cried because Lazarus had died, and the next minute He raised Lazarus from the dead because He was God.

One minute He died on the cross as a man. A few days later He rose from the dead to live in heaven with His Father, God.

Jesus is the most unique person to ever exist on Earth, and He is the only person who ever existed before His own human existence.

He is super, He is holy, He is righteous, He is gracious, He is loving. He is man, and He's the one true Superman!

Let's get creative and each draw a picture of Jesus as the greatest superhero of all time!

JESUS CHRIST

SCRIPTURE READING: JOHN 3:16

How often do you see or take a selfie? We see people taking them everywhere, right? Guess what? Jesus is God's selfie. He is the exact picture of God Himself. By seeing and knowing Jesus, we see and know God the Father.

Today for Fun Friday, we're going to create a craft project that lists all the character qualities of Jesus and the different ways He shows us God.

(For this activity, gather supplies beforehand, including cardboard or construction paper, glue, and pens, crayons, or colored markers.) Create a picture frame using cardboard or construction paper. Then where the picture would go, write out or illustrate the different qualities of Jesus that reflect the Father. When you're done, you've just drawn God's reflection.

Now let's decide how we'll display this image. *(If your family has a social-media page, you could take a picture of the illustration and post it there. Or you could display it on your refrigerator to remind your family that Jesus reflects God, and you're to reflect Jesus.)* If Jesus is God's selfie, what are you? *(Encourage responses.)*

You're supposed to be a mirror of Jesus, reflecting Him and His love to others around you.

Can you be that today? In what ways?

REPENTANCE

SCRIPTURE READING: 2 CHRONICLES 7:14

Whenever you're scheduled to go to the dentist, do you spend extra time brushing and flossing your teeth to impress him or her?

Do you think you can brush away a cavity the morning of a dentist appointment? Why or why not? Usually a cavity is deep within a tooth. Sometimes you can't even see it when you look at your tooth. Do you know how a dentist finds a cavity? Most of the time it's found with an X-ray. Have you ever had an X-ray of your teeth? What did that feel like? Were you scared? Why or why not?

Cavities are problems deep within our teeth that we can't see on the outside. In some ways, that's like sin. We don't always see our sin because some of it is deep within our hearts—like pride or a judgmental spirit. Can you always see a proud heart?

Name some other sins in our hearts that we don't always see.

Do you think God sees the sins in our hearts? Why or why not? *(Encourage responses.)* God looks deep into our hearts and sees every sin. When we sin, He wants us to repent of our sins. Repenting is more than just saying, "I'm sorry" for something we've done; it means we also stop doing it.

Let's close in prayer, asking God to make us aware of the sins in our hearts, the ones that may be invisible to others and even ourselves but are visible to Him. Then let's ask Him to help us repent and change.

REPENTANCE

SCRIPTURE READING: 1 JOHN 1:9

This week we're learning about repentance. When we repent, we realize that we're going in the wrong direction, so we turn around and head in the right direction. Repenting of our sins means recognizing that we're doing something wrong and then deciding to turn around and do the right thing.

Repentance is more than an apology. It's an apology that is backed up with a change in behavior. That is, if you apologize but continue doing wrong, you haven't repented.

For today's discussion, let's genuinely apologize to one another. Is there anyone in our family you feel you should apologize to? How do you think things will change based on your apology? Do you need to apologize to God for anything right now? How will things change based on that apology?

Let's pray and ask God to help us understand the true meaning of repentance and to practice it when we should.

REPENTANCE

SCRIPTURE READING: ACTS 3:19

God's Word has a lot to say about the very important subject of repentance. For today's Wednesday in the Word, let's jump right in and discover His guidance for each of us.

I have swept away your transgressions like a cloud, and your sins like a mist. Return to Me, for I have redeemed you. ISAIAH 44:22

Tear your hearts, not just your clothes, and return to the LORD your God. For He is gracious and compassionate, slow to anger, rich in faithful love, and He relents from sending disaster. JOEL 2:13

Repent and turn back, so that your sins may be wiped out, that seasons of refreshing may come from the presence of the Lord. ACTS 3:19

If we confess our sins, He is faithful and righteous to forgive us our sins and to cleanse us from all unrighteousness. 1 JOHN 1:9

Let's spend some time today letting God know we're truly sorry for our sins. But remember, repentance is more than simply saying we're sorry. What else does it include? *(A change in behavior.)*

Will you make an effort this week, with the Holy Spirit's help, to stop sinning in a certain way? Perhaps it's a heart problem, such as having a bad attitude at school. Or disobedience, such as ignoring a chore you've been asked to do. Whatever it is, make it a priority to stop this sin. That's true repentance.

REPENTANCE

SCRIPTURE READING: LUKE 13:3

Twin sisters Kelsey and Kylar are almost two years old. There's one major difference between the two: how they respond to their own dirty diapers. When Kelsey has a dirty diaper, she just continues playing as if nothing is wrong. She would much rather play with her dolls and toys than have to stop to be cleaned up and changed.

Kylar, on the other hand, is the exact opposite of Kelsey. When she has a dirty diaper, she immediately runs to her mommy or daddy and says, "Stinky, stinky, stinky!" She wants to be changed immediately, and she won't stop trying to get her parents' attention until her diaper is changed and she's clean again.

Some people live their lives a lot like Kelsey. They're so comfortable in their sin that they're not even interested in changing. However, the Bible calls us as Christians to be like Kylar. That is, we need to recognize the sin in our lives and immediately repent of the dirt so that we can be cleaned up. Repenting doesn't just mean that we *want* to be cleaned up; it means that we'll keep insisting on being cleaned up until we're changed.

Let's play a game called Setting the Table to illustrate what repentance involves. First, we'll need a volunteer. That person will set the table the wrong way. You'll put cups where plates go and put forks where they don't belong. When you're finished, show everyone the wrong table setting.

After you've done this, practice repentance. It's more than just saying that the table is set wrong. It also involves taking everything off the table and then setting it the right way. Each of us will have a turn setting the table and practicing repentance. Then we'll talk about what we learned.

REPENTANCE

SCRIPTURE READING: ACTS 17:30

Repenting of sin can be compared to driving a car on an interstate highway. When you make a mistake and miss your exit, you have to turn around. So you must get off the interstate. That's like confessing your sin and admitting you're wrong. However, that's only part of the process. The next step is to cross over the overpass. This is like deciding you'll no longer repeat this particular sin, or at least you'll try not to do it. (No one is perfect!)

When you get back on the interstate, you're now driving in the opposite direction. In other words, you're heading in a brand new direction from the direction you were heading in before. Your choices will reflect your heart's desire not to sin, and they'll take you to a new destination that's entirely different from your original destination when you were on the path of sin.

As we've been learning this week, repentance is much more than a prayer telling God you're sorry. It's an entire change in your mind-set and your actions.

For Fun Friday, let's create a visual illustration of what happens when we repent. *(For this activity, you'll need a jar, food coloring, and bleach.)* One of us will fill a jar with water. Than another volunteer will put one drop of red food coloring in the water. That food coloring represents sin.

Do you see how the coloring spreads through the water and completely changes it?

Now I'll add a liberal amount of bleach to the water and stir. The bleach illustrates how God washes away our sins when we repent and makes our hearts clean again.

Let's close in prayer, thanking God for the way He cleanses us from sin.

KINGDOM

SCRIPTURE READING: MATTHEW 6:33

Every good coach has a game plan for his team. The team must learn his game plan and apply it for the best chance of winning the game. Sometimes it's hard to pick up a particular coach's game plan, particularly if it's highly technical and very detailed.

As in athletic games and sports, in Christianity we have a lot of players who have been drafted out of the pit of hell and into the kingdom of God. Just as some athletes try to tell their coach how to run his team, too many Christians spend their time trying to tell God how to run His kingdom.

God's response is that it's His kingdom, not ours. He has His own program. He has His own game plan and agenda. He has adopted us into His family to be part of that plan. Each of us can play a strategic part in the game of life for His kingdom and His glory, but only if we operate according to His game plan—His kingdom agenda.

God's kingdom agenda is the visible demonstration of His comprehensive rule over every area of life. That means God isn't just God on Sunday when we're in church. God wants to be God over every single part of our lives: every decision we make, every relationship we have, and even every thought we think. God's kingdom is wherever He rules. He sits as king over your heart and mine.

What is a kingdom? What is a king?

Let's pretend that one of us is the king right now. *(Choose one family member to be king and have him or her sit on a chair for a throne.)* How would you treat this king? When he or she says something, will you do it?

Let's act out situations where the king (remember, it's a good king) tells us what to do and we all do it!

KINGDOM

SCRIPTURE READING: 1 CORINTHIANS 4:20

This week we're learning about the kingdom of God. That's the place where God rules. He rules the heavens and the earth. And one day Jesus Christ will return to Earth and take His place as king. He will set up His kingdom, and you and I will rule with Him. That's right! Jesus wants us to rule with Him when His kingdom comes.

However, Jesus will only allow those who believe in Him and live for Him the opportunity to participate in His future kingdom. The way you get into His kingdom is by believing in Him and allowing Him to forgive your sins. The way you get to participate in His kingdom after you're saved is by living your life for Him.

Today we're going to learn and recite the Lord's Prayer together. Let's practice until we have it memorized.

Our Father in heaven,
Hallowed be Your name.
Your kingdom come.
Your will be done
On earth as it is in heaven.
Give us this day our daily bread.
And forgive us our debts,
As we forgive our debtors.
And do not lead us into temptation,
But deliver us from the evil one.
For Yours is the kingdom and the power and the glory forever.
Amen.

MATTHEW 6:9–13, NKJV

KINGDOM

SCRIPTURE READING: ROMANS 14:17–18

When Jesus' followers asked Him to tell them who was the greatest in the kingdom, Jesus pulled a child close to Him and replied, "Whoever humbles himself like this child—this one is the greatest in the kingdom of heaven. And whoever welcomes one child like this in My name welcomes Me" (Matthew 18:4–5).

That's right. A child is the greatest in God's kingdom. Did you know that? Today's Wednesday in the Word passage tells us this is true. Why do you think Jesus said that? How does that make you feel? Does it make you happy to know that as a child, you are very special to God?

Sometimes we want to grow up fast. But remember, as you grow up it's good to keep these verses hidden in your heart. God wants you to remain a child in many ways, especially when it comes to having faith in Him.

Do you believe God makes miracles? Why or why not? What is a miracle?

God loves it when we believe in His power. After all, He's a great king. Let's take a moment right now to praise Him for being so big and powerful and for loving children as He does.

KINGDOM

SCRIPTURE READING: 1 CORINTHIANS 6:9–10

The White House in Washington, DC, has rules and regulations that must be followed whenever anyone steps into that house. When you enter the White House, you have to be checked and screened and walk through metal detectors. You're not allowed to wander off and touch anything in the White House if the governing staff hasn't granted you full permission.

The people who work in the White House also have to follow certain rules. Everything is done a certain way, at a certain time, for a certain purpose. This is because the president of the United States lives in the White House.

The kingdom of God is much like the White House. But the reality is that God's kingdom is even greater than the White House. God is the ruler of His kingdom. He rules over much more than the United States of America; He runs the entire universe.

Since we're living in God's kingdom, we must make sure we're following His rules. If we want to benefit from the kingdom of God and experience all that His kingdom has for us, then we must treat it with respect. Those who don't respect the kingdom of God won't be able to benefit from it, inherit it, or enter it.

In what ways can we show respect for God as king and for His kingdom?

Do you think the way we treat animals or nature shows respect or disrespect for God, since He created both? How do you think God would like us to treat them?

KINGDOM

SCRIPTURE READING: MATTHEW 10:7–8

D o you know the Pledge of Allegiance? Let's say it together.

I pledge allegiance to the flag of the United States of America, and to the Republic for which it stands, one Nation under God, indivisible, with liberty and justice for all.

Just as we need to be regularly reminded of our citizenship in this kingdom called America, we need to be reminded that we're also citizens of another kingdom—a greater and more perfect kingdom That kingdom is the kingdom of God.

A kingdom always includes three things: (1) a ruler, (2) people who live under that ruler, and (3) the rules. God's kingdom and His rule are over all.

For our Fun Friday activity, let's each write out a pledge to God and His kingdom. Spend some time making it just like you think it should be. When you're finished, hang it up somewhere or share it with others. You could even record yourself saying your pledge and post it online.

DISCIPLINE

SCRIPTURE READING: HEBREWS 12:11

Chores. Uh-oh. This probably isn't a subject you're excited about, right?

Chores may not be fun, but they're good, not only because they get things done, but also because they teach us valuable lessons—especially in the areas of personal discipline and responsibility.

Responsibility is critical when it come to accomplishing things we want to—whether in sports, starring in a school play, creating a drawing, or scoring a good grade on a test. To reach these goals, we have to be responsible. And to become responsible, we need to exercise our "responsibility muscle." One way to do this is by regularly completing our chores.

Learning to do chores is practicing the process of starting something and finishing it. You never want to do your chores halfway. A halfway-completed chore doesn't count. What if you made your bed only halfway? Would that count as making your bed? I don't think so.

(If your family has a chore chart, review it together and discuss how well each family member does completing the items on it. Then ask, "Is there room for improvement in doing your chores? Why or why not?"

If you don't have a family chore chart, create one together. Start by listing the different things your family needs to get done each week and then dividing the chores between family members. You can make it into a fancy chart if you want to. It doesn't have to look boring.)

Remember, chores are good because they teach us self-discipline and personal responsibility. What benefits can you expect from developing these qualities both now and in the future? *(Discuss.)*

DISCIPLINE

SCRIPTURE READING: PROVERBS 12:1

This week we're learning about discipline. It takes discipline to do the things we don't always like to do. In this house we can practice discipline in a very practical way. That means we're going to talk a little more about chores!

Every family member has certain chores to do around the house. That's just part of living in a household. If you live in our home and benefit from having a roof over your head, food on the table, heat in the winter, and a place to sleep at night, you should be more than happy to participate in doing family chores.

What does this have to do with our study of discipline? Let's consider our role model, Jesus Christ. He called Himself a servant. He often chose the difficult path for the good of others. He exercised discipline in that way. He cared for us through His sacrifice on the cross. In the same way, we can care for one another by sacrificing our time and energy to do things for our family.

For today's family activity, we're all going to pick different chores we can do right now to show that we're grateful for our home. What chores demonstrate the goodness of God in your life as part of our family?

When we're finished, we'll close in prayer, thanking God for the gift of our home and for His care. Let's share our thankfulness with Him.

DISCIPLINE

SCRIPTURE READING: PROVERBS 13:24

A boy was riding his bike around the block. Around and around he went, crying as he pedaled. A policeman saw him and said, "Son, where are you going?"

The boy replied, "I'm running away from home!"

The policeman pointed out that the boy hadn't even crossed the street.

The boy replied, "Yeah, I know I haven't crossed the street. I can't. My mom told me I'm not allowed to!"

In spite of his desire to run away, this little boy had enough personal discipline to obey the rules that kept him safe.

Personal discipline means choosing to behave the right way even when you don't feel like it. Maybe that relates to your chores—like picking up your room or emptying the dishwasher when you don't want to. Or maybe it just means keeping your mouth closed when you feel like lashing out at someone in your home. Whatever the case, you need to be able to discipline yourself to live a Christlike life.

Children often think of discipline as something their parents do to them. But true discipline is demonstrated by controlling your temper, your desires, or even your thoughts to keep your heart and actions pure before God and others. Learning to control yourself will save you from a world of trouble down the road.

For today's Wednesday in the Word, let's do an Internet search on "self-discipline Bible verses." Then we'll look up and read some of the Bible passages that come up in the search results. *(If you don't have Internet access, look up a few of these passages in your Bible: Psalms 119:9–11 and 141:3; 1 Corinthians 8:13 and 9:24–27; Philippians 3:12–14.)*

DISCIPLINE

SCRIPTURE READING: 1 CORINTHIANS 9:27

Ant mounds are full of worker ants. These ants have several jobs to help take care of the nest. Worker ants must care for the queen and the baby ants. They defend the nest to keep the entire colony safe. And they must leave the nest to find food for the other ants. Doing their jobs ensures that the entire nest runs successfully.

Without worker ants, the queen ant wouldn't be able to lay eggs safely. The baby ants wouldn't be able to survive, and the colony would go hungry. The worker ants benefit from their own work, and without them, the colony would be in trouble.

As a family, we can learn a lot from worker ants. It's good if everyone has a job to do in our home, since each of us benefits from living here. It isn't right to benefit from sharing a home and not have any responsibilities to help keep the home functioning.

What are some ways you can be more helpful around the house or at school? Are you willing to do these things on a regular basis? Remember, you'll need to use discipline to accomplish what needs to be done. You may not always feel like doing what's needed, but with God's help, you can!

DISCIPLINE

SCRIPTURE READING: PROVERBS 3:11–12

Have you ever seen those punching bags you can knock down? When you knock one down, it bounces back up. You can slam it to the ground or kick it, and—*boom!*—it comes right back up. The only way you can keep the punching bag from coming back up is to destroy it.

The reason the bag comes back up is because there's a weight at its base. The weight forces whatever external pressure you put on it to bring the bag right back up. That's a lot like biblical discipline. No matter what your circumstances or your situation is . . . *bang! bing!* Back up!

Your ability to recover from life's blows is that "weight" on the inside of the punching bag. It's the discipline you exercise to overcome grumpiness, grouchiness, laziness, or even a rebellious spirit when it comes to chores or obedience or arguing or complaining. But by yourself, you don't have that kind of personal discipline.

When external pressures in life knock you down, you're able to bounce back—that's the power of God's Spirit supporting you. This enables you to overcome things that cause you to be emotionally challenged.

Personal discipline is an important part of living life to the fullest. For today's Fun Friday activity, let's practice personal discipline by seeing who can keep his or her mouth shut the longest. That probably doesn't sound fun. But the fun part is that you can try to make a family member laugh or talk while that person tries to keep his or her mouth shut. *(Time each person for three minutes while everyone else tries to get him or her to laugh or talk.)*

The Urban Alternative

D r. Tony Evans' ministry The Urban Alternative (TUA) *equips, empowers,* and *unites* Christians to impact *individuals, families, churches,* and *communities* through a thoroughly Kingdom agenda worldview. In teaching truth, we seek to transform lives.

The core cause of the problems we face in our personal lives, homes, churches, and societies is a spiritual one; therefore, the only way to address it is spiritually. We've tried a political, social, economic, and even a religious agenda.

It's time for a *Kingdom agenda.*

The Kingdom agenda can be defined as the visible manifestation of the comprehensive rule of God over every area of life.

The unifying central theme throughout the Bible is the glory of God and the advancement of His kingdom. The conjoining thread from Genesis to Revelation—from beginning to end—is focused on one thing: God's glory through advancing God's kingdom.

When you do not have that theme, the Bible becomes disconnected stories that are great for inspiration but seem to be unrelated in purpose and direction. The Bible exists to share God's movement in history toward the establishment and expansion of His kingdom highlighting the connectivity throughout which is the kingdom. Understanding that increases the relevancy of this several-thousand-year-old manuscript to your day-to-day living, because the kingdom is not only then, it is now.

The absence of the kingdom's influence in our personal and family lives, churches, and communities has led to a deterioration in our world of immense proportions:

- People live segmented, compartmentalized lives because they lack God's kingdom worldview.
- Families disintegrate because they exist for their own satisfaction rather than for the kingdom.

The TETC program includes courses for both local and online students. Furthermore, TETC programming includes course work for non-student attendees. Pastors, Christian leaders, and Christian laity, both local and at a distance, can seek out The Kingdom Agenda Certificate for personal, spiritual, and professional development. Some courses are valued for CEU credit as well as viable in transferring for college credit with our partner school(s).

Kingdom Agenda Pastors (KAP) provides a viable network for like-minded pastors who embrace the Kingdom agenda philosophy. Pastors have the opportunity to go deeper with Dr. Tony Evans as they are given greater biblical knowledge, practical applications, and resources to impact individuals, families, churches, and communities. KAP welcomes senior and associate pastors of all churches. KAP also offers an annual Summit held each year in Dallas with intensive seminars, workshops, and resources.

Pastors' Wives Ministry, founded by Dr. Lois Evans, provides counsel, encouragement, and spiritual resources for pastors' wives as they serve with their husbands in the ministry. A primary focus of the ministry is the KAP Summit that offers senior pastors' wives a safe place to reflect, renew, and relax along with training in personal development, spiritual growth, and care for their emotional and physical well-being.

COMMUNITY IMPACT

National Church Adopt-A-School Initiative (NCAASI) prepares churches across the country to impact communities by using public schools as the primary vehicle for effecting positive social change in urban youth and families. Leaders of churches, school districts, faith-based organizations, and other nonprofit organizations are equipped with the knowledge and tools to forge partnerships and build strong social service delivery systems. This training is based on the comprehensive church-based community impact strategy conducted by Oak Cliff Bible Fellowship. It addresses such areas as economic development, education, housing, health revitalization, family renewal, and racial reconciliation. We assist churches in tailoring the model to meet specific needs of their communities while simultaneously addressing the spiritual and moral frame of reference. Training events are held annually in the Dallas area at Oak Cliff Bible Fellowship.

Athlete's Impact (AI) exists as an outreach both into and through the sports arena. Coaches are the most influential factor in young people's lives, even ahead of their parents. With the growing rise of fatherlessness in our culture, more young people are looking to their coaches for guidance, character development, practical needs, and hope. Athletes are next on the influencer scale after coaches. Athletes (whether professional or amateur) influence younger athletes and kids within their spheres of impact. Knowing this, we have made it our aim to equip and train coaches and athletes on how to live out and utilize their God-given roles for the benefit of the kingdom. We aim to do this through our iCoach App, weCoach Football Conference as well as resources such as *The Playbook: A Life Strategy Guide for Athletes.*

RESOURCE DEVELOPMENT

We are fostering lifelong learning partnerships with the people we serve by providing a variety of published materials. Dr. Evans has published more than one hundred unique titles based on over forty years of preaching, whether that is in booklet, book, or Bible study format. The goal is to strengthen individuals in their walk with God and service to others.

☙

For more information and a complimentary copy of Dr. Evans' devotional newsletter,

call (800) 800-3222;

or write TUA at PO Box 4000, Dallas TX 75208;

or visit us online at www.TonyEvans.org.

ABOUT THE AUTHORS

DR. TONY EVANS is one of the country's most respected leaders in evangelical circles. As a pastor, teacher, author, and speaker, he serves the body of Christ through his unique ability to communicate complex theological truth through simple, yet profound, illustrations.

Dr. Evans has served as the senior pastor of Oak Cliff Bible Fellowship for close to four decades, and also serves as the founder and president of The Urban Alternative. He seeks to restore hope and transform lives through the proclamation and the application of the Word of God. His daily radio broadcast, *The Urban Alternative with Dr. Tony Evans*, can be heard on nearly 1,000 radio outlets throughout the United States and in more than 130 countries.

He has written more than 100 books, including the best-selling *Kingdom Man* and *Kingdom Woman* (written with his daughter Chrystal).

He has been married to Lois, his wife and ministry partner of over forty years. They are the proud parents of four children and the proud grandparents of twelve and great-grandparents of one.

JONATHAN EVANS, an author, speaker, and former NFL fullback, treasures his relationship with Christ along with the opportunity to use his life to glorify God. Jonathan seeks to impact today's athletes, men, and young adults by equipping and encouraging them in their faith.

Jonathan is a graduate of Dallas Theological Seminary with a master's degree in christian leadership.

He serves as the chaplain of the Dallas Cowboys and cochaplain of the Dallas Mavericks.

He is the coauthor of *Get in the Game: A Spiritual Workout for Athletes*. Jonathan is a dynamic speaker at churches, conferences, men's events, banquets, youth activities, and events affiliated with the Fellowship of Christian Athletes. He is committed to developing the next generation of devoted Christian leaders.

Jonathan and his wife, Kanika, are the proud parents of Kelsey, Jonathan II, Kamden, and Kylar.